Reporter in Red China

Reporter

in Red China

by CHARLES TAYLOR

RANDOM HOUSE New York

FIRST PRINTING

© Copyright, 1966, by Charles Taylor
All rights reserved under International and Pan-American Copyright Conventions. Published in New York by Random House, Inc., and simultaneously in Toronto, Canada, by Random House of Canada Limited.

Library of Congress Catalog Card Number: 66–23497

Manufactured in the United States of America by American Book–Stratford Press, Inc.

The author is grateful to the following for permission to quote:

The Hoover Institution for *Communist China: The Politics of Student Opposition* by Dennis J. Doolin.

Frederick A. Praeger, Inc., for *The New Class: An Analysis of the Communist System* by Milovan Djilas, and *The Political Thought of Mao Tse-Tung* by Stuart R. Schram.

Columbia University Press for *Oriental Civilizations: Sources of Chinese Tradition* by Wm. Theodore de Bary.

Archon Books, The Shoe String Press, Inc., and Longmans, Green & Co. Ltd., for *An Embassy to China*, J. L. Cranmer-Byng, ed.

All photographs by the author, courtesy *The Globe and Mail* (Toronto).

Book designed by Victoria Dudley

To my Peking friends

"Every perfect traveller always creates the country
where he travels."

—NIKOS KAZANTZAKIS

"Nothing could be more fallacious than to judge
of China by any European standard."

—LORD MACARTNEY
First British Ambassador to China

Introduction

THIS BOOK is the result of eighteen months spent in China as resident correspondent for the Toronto *Globe and Mail.* I was based in Peking from May, 1964, to October, 1965, as one of four correspondents from the West, and the only North American.

There is no shortage of books on China, but most are either scholarly works written from the outside or the reports of visitors who have had the standard short tour; books by residents are rare. This one is written in the belief that the experience of a resident yields information and insights which may be of interest to both the specialist and the general reader.

I have not tried to cover every aspect of contemporary China. Instead, I have concentrated on subjects which interest me and which I consider important: the atmosphere of Peking, the outlook of the younger generation, the political techniques of the leaders, and the treatment of foreigners, among others.

As a political reporter, I reach certain conclusions and make certain predictions. But I have tried to avoid moral judgments. For even if a foreigner knows something of Chinese history and Chinese psychology, he can never *feel* as a Chinese feels, and without that basic empathy, judgment is both futile and presumptuous.

Contents

1

Foreign Correspondents— Our Life and Hard Times

It was four o'clock in the morning and across Peking telephones were ringing in the homes of about thirty foreign correspondents. Unless he rolled over in the bed and went back to sleep—which often happened—the correspondent who staggered to the phone heard a familiar voice, intoning a ritual summons in an appropriate tongue (usually English, French, Russian, or Japanese): "This is the Information Department of the Foreign Ministry. We will be issuing a piece of news in fifteen minutes."

Always alert and terribly awake, that voice had it all over the correspondent, still struggling out of his sleep. Sometimes scornfully, sometimes apologetically, it refused to divulge the subject matter of the "piece of news" (nor did it ever offer any explanation of why the Chinese Foreign Ministry deems it appropriate to issue many of its communiqués in the middle of the night).

All this placed the correspondent in a terrible dilemma. He knew that if he put on some clothes and conscientiously rushed to the Foreign Ministry, he would certainly be presented with a statement of the most minimal interest to his readers—perhaps an announcement that China and some small African nation were establishing diplomatic relations, or a routine Chinese complaint over events in Laos. But he also knew that if he shrugged his way back under the bedclothes, he would inevitably miss the announcement of a Chinese atomic test, a new protest to the Americans or the Russians, or some other sure-fire front-page item.

Usually the Information Department rang once, and then left the correspondent to struggle with his conscience. On this occasion, however, the Chinese seemed especially pleased with their piece of news (it was one of their warnings to India during the Indo–Pakistan war of 1965) and kept on phoning one bedroom—mine—at steady intervals for an hour, without success. Finally, in desperation, they phoned a colleague, who was fortunately awake and working on his story. Just where could Mr. Taylor be, at four o'clock in the morning, the voice asked plaintively and with obvious bewilderment, if not in his own bed? My colleague, who had a shrewd idea, tactfully pleaded ignorance.

This incident may speak little for my zeal as a correspondent (although my editor, a civilized man, always allowed that a one-man bureau could not keep a twenty-four-hour alert, especially when that one man was a bachelor, and since, among the foreign community in Peking, there were some attractive ladies). But it is as good an example as any of how the Information Department and I failed to understand each other.

Although conducted within a façade of elaborate courtesy, relations between the Information Department and most foreign correspondents in Peking are usually in a state of undeclared hostility, for one outstanding reason: the vast gulf between our different conceptions of how a newsman operates. It is our job to secure information and report it to our readers. It is their job to withhold most significant information, while flooding us with the greatest possible amount of propaganda. If we both do our jobs honestly, our confrontation brooks no compromise.

It would be wise at the start to explode some popular misconceptions held by many in the outside world. In scores of conversations I have encountered one general view of the foreign correspondents in Peking—that we are a small, embattled, and embittered band, subject to the most rigid censorship, unable to travel, and under orders from our editors to write nothing critical of the Chinese, for fear of instant expulsion. Actually our situation is much more complex, rather less gloomy, and at times even amusing.

Roughly thirty foreign correspondents are resident in Peking—about fifteen from the Soviet Union and Eastern Europe, nine Japanese, and a scattering of individuals from Cuba, North Korea, North Vietnam, and the South Vietnamese National Liberation Front; finally, there are four from the West, representing the British, French, and West German news agencies, and the Toronto *Globe and Mail*. Although there is a rumor that one day we will all be housed together, at present we are scattered around Peking—two have houses, a few live in their embassies, and the rest inhabit hotels or the apartment compounds built for foreigners.

There is no censorship—for this, the Chinese deserve some credit, especially when their methods are compared with those of other totalitarian states. Whatever their subject, our cables are scanned briefly for typing mistakes and then promptly dispatched. During my eighteen months in Peking, I sent several hundred thousand words by cable and air mail, and every word got through. As a special concession to correspondents I was also able to ship film that was unprocessed and, therefore, unviewed by the Chinese authorities.

We assume that our cables are read as they go out, and we know that the Chinese receive our newspapers and news services. Sometimes, when a story offends, its author is later summoned to the Foreign Ministry, lectured more in sorrow than in anger, and perhaps given a "serious warning." But only a tiny handful of correspondents have ever been expelled, although in recent years several have offended mightily, myself included. In this the Chinese seem more tolerant than the Russians (although they are also free from the problem of uninhibited American reporters). Correspondents from other Communist countries, friendly or hostile, are obviously a special case, governed entirely by political considerations. Politics also plays a part in the treatment of correspondents from the West and Japan, but each of us is in Peking in exchange for a Chinese correspondent in our own country, and I suspect that the Chinese are reluctant to risk any reciprocal action against their own men.

As far as I know none of the Western correspondents is under orders from his office to exercise restraint, in spite of the rare value of a Peking dateline. (On taking up my post, I had no such instructions, and when I later ran afoul of the Chinese authorities, my editors backed me to the hilt.) Generally we try to function as newsmen, guided only by our normal standards of accuracy and good taste. There was only one subject upon which I ever imposed voluntary self-censorship: the health of the leaders, especially Mao Tse-tung. On this subject Chinese officials are abnormally sensitive, and it is probably unwise for the correspondent to relay the rumors of the diplomatic cocktail circuit. (Making idle conversation at an airport reception, a colleague once remarked that Chen Yi, the burly Foreign Minister, was walking without the cane that he often carries. Blazing with anger, an Information Department official turned on the correspondent and accused him of slandering the People's Republic of China.) More often, in fact, it is the *visiting* correspondents—those who enter China for the standard two-month tour—who exercise restraint. While there are many honorable exceptions, some seem determined to write nothing that will hinder their chances for another visa. In this sense the residents are much freer than the visitors. Yet our freedom is only relative, and the nature of the job makes each day a rather dreary round.

Living in the Hsin Chiao, one of the three or four main hotels for foreigners, I was awakened each morning by the high-pitched chatter of Japanese businessmen, telephoning to Tokyo to report the progress of their negotiations with the Chinese state trading corporations, and apparently convinced that it helped to shout. With practice I managed to time my ablutions so that I reached the dining room at precisely nine o'clock, the deadline for breakfast. Equally skilled, my West German colleague would arrive at the same time. There would ensue a gloomy half-hour, during which we picked at our indifferent eggs and sausages, cautiously sipped the rather startling coffee, compared the severity of our hangovers, fondly anticipated our next holiday in Hong Kong, exchanged gossip from the diplomatic community, and commiserated with each other about the lack of any hard news. Then, when it could be postponed no longer, we would descend to our offices and our translators, and the work would begin.

Mostly, work meant reading. For correspondents in China the basic sources of information are the English-language service of Hsinhua (the New China News Agency) and a half dozen Peking newspapers. Aside from predictably slanted foreign news and cheerful domestic items about happy peasants and striking economic progress, Hsinhua carries all major policy statements of the Chinese government and the Chinese Communist Party. From the newspapers, which we scanned with our translators, we derived items that were more detailed, and often more revealing. These newspapers range from the august Peking *People's Daily,* the six-page voice of the Central Committee of the Chinese Communist Party, to those which concentrate on local items, economic matters, and even sports, or which address themselves to intellectuals, workers, or young people.

Most of this is the worst sort of chaff, and conveys the picture of a never-never land of which only a Baden-Powell could possibly approve. On all sides workers, peasants, and intellectuals are bursting with good intentions and solemn resolve, avidly reading the works of Chairman Mao, helping their fellow men, and leading earnest lives of great frugality and high endeavor. Nearly everything, it seems, is for the best in what will soon become the best of all possible worlds. The darker side of life is resolutely ignored, and if such things exist in China as murders or other crimes of passion, you would never know it from the Chinese press.

And yet the newspapers can often be remarkably revealing. To a large extent they are a major means by which the Party conveys its directives to the people, and especially to the cadres. Often they herald important new campaigns. In the summer of 1964 an inside page of the *People's Daily* was devoted for several weeks to attacks on a leading philosopher, Yang Hsien-chen. For many days few correspondents or diplomats paid much attention to these abstruse arguments, which were concerned with the pressing dialectical problem of whether "one divides into two" or "two divides into one." To us it all seemed like so many angels on the point of a needle. Eventually, however, it became apparent that Yang was under attack for preaching class reconciliation and Soviet-style revisionism. As it turned out, we were witnessing the start of an intensive campaign against intellectuals and artists which subse-

quently claimed dozens of important scapegoats and cul-
minated in the sweeping purge of mid-1966.

Once you learn to read them properly, the newspapers
often reveal areas of resistance to the regime or examples
of policies that have backfired. It was obvious that the
drive to send young city-dwellers to settle in the countryside was running into trouble when Peking newspapers
began printing articles from enthusiastic parents, stating
how happy they were to send their children out on such a
noble task. If many parents had not been complaining,
there would have been no need for such eulogies. For
several weeks in the summer of 1965 the newspapers
urged all young Chinese to follow the example of China's
most famous swimmer, Mao Tse-tung, and throw themselves into lakes and rivers in order to build their bodies
and increase their ability to defend the homeland. Each
day articles told how hundreds in one locality and thousands in another were joyfully responding to the call.
Suddenly, two or three weeks after the campaign began, a
rash of articles appeared on water safety, giving detailed
instructions on artificial respiration. Since nothing in the
Chinese press appears by chance, it was clear that, in an
excess of zeal, thousands of youngsters were hurling
themselves into turbulent waters and thoroughly drowning.

With Hsinhua, too, we learned to read between the
lines. As in other Communist countries, but perhaps to an
even greater extent, the Chinese weigh carefully the value
of every phrase and slogan, and the slightest change is
always significant. It can have great meaning if a slogan
drops from use or another takes its place. Sometimes a
single new word can herald or confirm an important
trend, as when the Chinese added "prudent" to the list of
adjectives describing their forthcoming Third Five Year
Plan. And when a government statement raises the possibility of sending Chinese troops to Vietnam, the conscien-

tious correspondent must scrutinize every qualifying phrase as carefully as it was selected by its authors.

No newsman is happy to rely on such academic sources. We like to see with our own eyes, to talk directly to senior officials, to describe events as they happen. In this we were almost constantly frustrated, for it is the clear Chinese contention that no news exists until it has been printed in the *People's Daily*, and that there is then nothing more to add. Nothing could be better, from their point of view, than what happened at the important Communist Youth League conference, held in Peking in June, 1964, which was addressed by senior leaders and which laid down major new policy guidelines. Yet although thirty-three hundred delegates and observers came to Peking for the conference and their deliberations lasted for more than a week, only the vaguest rumors among the foreign community indicated that something unusual might be afoot. It was not until several days after the conference had closed, when newspapers suddenly splashed the news and pictures across their front pages, that we definitely knew what had happened.

In similar secrecy China's so-called parliament, the National People's Congress, meets in Peking for a few weeks at irregular intervals. During its deliberations correspondents are physically prevented by police from coming within a hundred yards of the Great Hall of the People, and from the nearly three thousand delegates there is seldom a leak that reaches the foreign community. Virtually our only source of information on the National People's Conference is an official transcript, highly abridged, of the keynote speech by Prime Minister Chou En-lai.

Nor is it any help to seek out Chinese officials. It is no use phoning directly to some government department, since all requests must be channeled through the Information Department. Interviews can sometimes be arranged, after considerable delay, and Information Department officials say they are available for briefings. But a correspondent's hopes are quickly dashed, for such interviews and briefings are almost entirely useless, since they simply repeat, in almost identical words, the latest government statement or *People's Daily* editorial. Here, too, the gap in understanding seems too wide to bridge, for the Chinese officials seem genuinely trying to be helpful. When a correspondent complains that he is getting the same regurgitated pap and no real news, the official will react with apparent concern and even pain—"Sometimes, Mr. Taylor, we feel your attitude is not exactly friendly."

Only very rarely will one of the more sophisticated and less timid officials venture beyond his brief. Once, at a state banquet in the Great Hall of the People, I had a long conversation with a Foreign Ministry man on the subject of Taiwan. On this subject the Chinese feel most passionately of all, for they hold that the island is an integral part of China and that only the "occupation" by American forces prevents its return to the mainland. Speaking with great fervor, my tablemate suddenly burst out, "You must remember this about Taiwan—*we* are the oppressed!" This, stated with considerable emotion, seemed genuinely spontaneous.

There are some hopeful signs that the Chinese may slowly be adapting their methods of handling the foreign press. In September, 1965, Foreign Minister Chen Yi held a mammoth press conference for several hundred resident and visiting correspondents. It was virtually without precedent and yielded important new policy statements on nearly a dozen key issues. Just as important for us, it was a highly colorful occasion, with the old marshal bellowing with rage, chortling at his own jokes, growling in his rough Szechwan accent, and using vivid expressions rarely found in Hsinhua. On that day we functioned as real newsmen, and it can only be hoped that the Chinese will consider the experiment worth repeating.

For those correspondents from the Soviet Union and other "revisionist" countries, frustrations are different but just as acute. Unlike the Westerners, they can subscribe to provincial newspapers, which often reveal interesting details about local conditions. They also receive a daily bulletin of limited circulation, similar to those distributed among the more trusted Chinese cadres, which contains Western news reports of world events and even the edited version of some of our own dispatches from Peking. But these are the only lingering privileges to survive the full onslaught of the Sino–Soviet dispute. In terms of access to news and high officials, the Communists are no better off than their Western colleagues.

At least the Western correspondent has the satisfaction of seeing his work in print. Almost nothing written by the Communists is ever carried by their newspapers and news agencies. As one of them asked scornfully, "Why should we give them any publicity?" Instead, the Communist correspondent in Peking sends restricted reports that are usually read only by a limited circle of Party members in his country.

With the exception of our Albanian colleague, who seems to lead a rather isolated life, most of the Communist correspondents from the Soviet Union and Eastern Europe regard the Sino–Soviet dispute as an extremely tragic event. Few find it easy to speak of the Chinese actions with anything but bitterness, and some take it very hard indeed. It is probably much easier for the Western correspondents to disregard the daily fulminations against "imperialism" than it is for the Communists to ignore the unending polemics against "modern revisionism." Some manage to be vastly amused by the larger lunacies in the Chinese press (many, I often felt, would have little trouble securing a job with Radio Armenia). But most are often as indignant as the colleague who told me angrily: "I've been a Communist for forty years, and gone to jail several times. And now my interpreter, a kid in his early twenties, tells me that I don't understand Marxism–Leninism!"

If he wanted only a quiet life, the Western reporter would be advised to follow the instructions that Confucius gave to a disciple who asked how to conduct himself in politics:

> Hear much, but leave to one side that which is doubtful, and speak with due caution concerning the remainder; in this way you will seldom incur blame. See much, but leave to one side that of which the meaning is not clear, and act carefully with regard to the rest; thus you will have few occasions for regret.

Perhaps such advice is only practical when dealing with the double difficulties posed by a closed Communist society and a Chinese culture that is so foreign and baffling to most Europeans. But in fact a Western newsman does his best to overcome the obstacles. In short, he seeks the news. And it can be done, because not even the Chinese are able to block all sources of information. Aside from rumors that reach the embassies through various channels, scraps of news can be picked up from foreign students, teachers, and other experts who have closer contact with the Chinese. Lucky in my sources, I was able to break to the outside world two major stories—Ssu Ching and the Great Painting Hoax—which the Chinese did their best to cover up.

In the autumn of 1964 word started reaching me that a strange exodus was taking place from Peking. Thousands of Party officials, office workers, and students were leaving the capital for the countryside; whole classes at Peking University had gone out. This was some new campaign, quite different from the regular drive which sends city-dwellers to work on the communes for about a month each year. In this case, it was said, they would be gone for eight to ten months.

Slowly the story began to fall into place. Not only Peking but other cities were sending their citizens to the communes; perhaps it was happening in every part of China. At any rate the poorer provinces were certainly target areas—from Heilungkiang in former Manchuria, to Shantung on the Yellow Sea, and Yunnan in the extreme southwest. At least hundreds of thousands of city-dwellers were involved, and one report said two million. Their mission: to live with the peasants and to root out tyranny and corruption on the part of commune managers and other officials.

According to one version I heard, it all started when Wang Kuang-mei, wife of head of state Liu Shao-chi, went incognito to a commune for her bout of physical labor. As she later reported to her husband and Chairman Mao, corruption was widespread among Party leaders on the communes. In fear of reprisals the peasants dared not speak. The delinquents could be uncovered only if trusted Party members were sent to the communes from other areas, to live there for a long time and slowly establish the truth.

Whatever its origins, the campaign was a major drive of huge proportions aimed at corrupt and greedy officials. They were charged with allotting themselves and their cronies too many work points, with stealing commune produce and embezzling commune funds, and with running illicit wine presses and other black market enterprises. Some were ruling their communes like warlords of old, with many of the attendant vices. Some, it was even said, were selecting the prettiest peasant girls for their private harems.

The name of this campaign was Ssu Ching, or Four Cleanouts, a typical Chinese title for a typical mass campaign (each of the four points was a paragraph of crimes). Since it aimed at nothing less than preserving for the Party the loyalty of the peasants (on whom the Communists had based their revolution), it was a movement of tremendous importance. It was widely discussed among the Chinese people, yet in conversations with foreigners only a very few Chinese would dare to acknowledge the existence of Ssu Ching. Nothing about it was appearing in the press, and when I phoned the Information Department to request a briefing, they told me blandly that they had no idea what I was talking about.

Still, I wrote the story, and it received wide distribution in the West; it was later confirmed through information patiently collected by the China-watchers in Hong Kong. My story can hardly have pleased the Chinese, although in the writing of it I more or less implied my sympathy for their aims. Yet they neither objected nor called me on the carpet, perhaps because Ssu Ching had become too widespread for its existence to be denied.

I was less lucky with the Great Painting Hoax.

On a cold and windy morning in January, 1965, one of my best sources came to my hotel. As we sat sipping coffee in the bar upstairs, he related a remarkable tale. It concerned a painting, "You Lead, I Follow," by a young artist, Li Tse-hao. This painting had been shown at an exhibition in Peking, praised by the critics, and reproduced in full color on the back cover of the last 1964 issue of *China Youth,* a nationally distributed magazine for young people. In the approved style of socialist realism it showed cheerfully smiling young peasants surging through a wheat field and bringing in the harvest.

Then, after the magazine had reached all parts of the country, a horrified official discovered that the painting was a gigantic hoax, filled with violent anti-Communist slogans and symbols. Two slogans in Chinese characters were cleverly concealed in the stubble of the wheat field: "Long Live Chiang Kai-shek" and "Kill Communists." Also hidden in the wheat were likenesses of Lenin and Chairman Mao, their bodies being trampled in the dust by the smiling peasants. In the distant background, more peasants could be seen as tiny figures marching along under three red banners. This seemed a clear allusion to a favorite Chinese slogan: "Hold Aloft the Three Red Banners of the Party's General Line, the Great Leap Forward, and the People's Communes." The second red banner had fallen to the ground—just as the Great Leap Forward itself had collapsed amid near calamity—knocked down by a wind blowing from the west, or left-hand, side of the painting, reversing one of Chairman Mao's favorite boasts: "The East wind is prevailing over the West wind."

When they discovered the hoax, officials called in all copies of *China Youth* from every school, library, and private home across the nation. According to my source, an inquiry had been launched and many were under suspicion. The artist and the editors of the magazine were being subjected to strenuous investigation but were protesting their innocence. At the same time, officials were forbidding public discussion of the scandal, especially with foreigners.

Discreetly approaching other sources, I discovered there was no doubt about the scandal (I later found out that the magazine had been recalled from as far away as the Communist bookstores in Hong Kong), but some people were still not certain whether the anti-Communist propaganda was intentional, or a series of remarkable coincidences, misinterpreted by suspicious and overimaginative minds.

After some searching I managed to secure a copy of the magazine. Knowing what to look for, I had no trouble spotting the figures of Mao and Lenin; the likenesses were excellent, although it was just possible that this was an extraordinary coincidence. I had less doubt about the fallen red banner: it was small, but unmistakably on the ground, and given the sensitivity of the Chinese to symbols and slogans, the allusion could hardly have been unconscious.

Finally, I showed the magazine to friends who were expert in the Chinese language. None was able to find the slogan "Kill Communists," but while one or two were uncertain, most had no trouble tracing out the five characters for "Long Live Chiang Kai-shek." They showed me how the characters were far from perfect reproductions, but too close to the originals to be coincidental. Some time later a China-hand in Hong Kong told me that when he first heard the news, he gave his copy of the magazine, to which he subscribed, to his Chinese assistant, telling him that there might be several unusual things concealed in the painting, but without giving details. Half an hour later the assistant returned, highly excited. On a piece of tracing paper laid over the painting, he had outlined all the slogans and symbols mentioned in my report.

To any Chinese this sort of hoax *is* highly exciting, for the Chinese mind delights in puns, jokes, subtle allusions, and trickery of every sort. Chinese history is filled with precedents for such a stunt, for through the centuries poets and painters have expressed their opposition to tyrannical dynasties by concealing slogans and double meanings in their work. In the closed society of Communist China it was especially audacious. Given the stringent supervision of mass communications, it was equally startling that the hoax had gone so far before it was detected.

At any rate, I had my story, and sent it off (for once I took no chances, and gave it to a friend to mail from Hong Kong). While stating that there was no doubt about the scandal, I wrote that it was just possible that all the propaganda was accidental, even though the evidence to the contrary seemed overwhelming. I added another qualification: that the hoax, if real, did not indicate a strong undercurrent of active opposition to the Communist regime or widespread support for Chiang Kai-shek, since neither existed to any significant degree. All it showed, I said, was that one individual had felt so oppressed by the stifling demands of the Communist state that he abandoned all caution to express his opposition in a reckless but traditional manner.

My newspaper splashed the story on its front page. News agencies picked it up and carried it around the world. It was a sensation on Taiwan, where Nationalist newspapers printed retouched reproductions of the painting which crudely exaggerated the anti-Communist propaganda. In Hong Kong, Nationalist supporters distributed the story as a broadsheet, while a pro-Communist newspaper tried to discredit the story, without acknowledging the scandal's existence, by announcing that the original painting was on exhibition in Canton (but travelers from Hong Kong who visited the exhibition said they found no trace of it, despite a careful search).

I had, of course, anticipated that the story would get me into trouble with Chinese officials and might provide the Kuomintang with propaganda. Neither possibility appealed to me, but as a newsman I had no choice—it was too good a story to ignore. Three weeks later I was summoned to the Foreign Ministry and confronted by two Information Department officials. One of these, a lady, read from a prepared text in Chinese, while the other interpreted in flawless Oxford English. I was told that my article had been written with political aims, called for subversive activities, and had been used by the Kuomintang as propaganda. What was more, it was totally untrue, since there had been no such scandal, the magazine had never been recalled, and "as for the artist, he paints as usual at his original post." I had exceeded my functions as a correspondent, they were giving me a warning, and they hoped that I would be more attentive in the future.

Of course, I stuck to my story and denied their charges. This only led them to repeat the whole indictment, almost word for word. It was a strange interview, sad and ludicrous. Since the story touched such a sensitive subject and had been so widely distributed, they were forced to deny it. At the same time I was certain that they knew that I knew that they knew that my facts were right. Yet the sorry farce had to be played out.

A few weeks later they found a way of telling their own people that there had never been any scandal. It was a very Chinese way, subtle and oblique. One day the *Peking Daily* simply reproduced the painting, without any stated reason, somewhat blurred and possibly retouched. In a lengthy caption an anonymous critic took great pains in praising the artistic manner in which the stalks of wheat had been portrayed, and said that the painting had won "rather good comments." As for the painter, another choice sentence stated that he had "recently returned from the countryside." In other words, the hoax and the scandal were non-events.

After that I was Number-One Bad Boy among the newsmen. In this I served a useful purpose, for the Chinese have a need for "negative examples," to use a favorite phrase of Chairman Mao's. When I first arrived in Peking, a Deputy Director of the Information Department had spent much time complaining to me about the dispatches of a distinguished French colleague—I was clearly meant to avoid his follies—and later arrivals were lectured in a similar way about my own excesses.

As much as anything else, this incident points up the great gulf between the working methods of a Western newsman and the Chinese conception of how we should operate. It was with evident pain and perplexity that the same Deputy Director would later tell my colleagues that he couldn't understand how Mr. Taylor could have made such a mistake. After all, he would say, I had spent a long time in China, and before that in Hong Kong, and I must know how sensitive the Chinese were to any mention of the Kuomintang. I think he genuinely failed to understand that to a Western reporter a story is a story, regardless of any political consequences.

It was also a good example of how resident correspondents are a constant worry and embarrassment to the Chinese, since by living in China for a period of time, we inevitably discover things that the authorities would prefer to keep hidden. I suspect that the Chinese greatly prefer visiting correspondents, however experienced and persevering. On the standard two-month tour, always following the same beaten track and always seeing the same factories and communes, they are much more easily shielded from the darker side of life in China. I am fairly certain that no Western newsmen would be allowed to live in China, were it not for the Chinese desire to have their own newsmen in our capitals.

A few weeks later the Chinese automatically renewed my credentials for another six-month period. After that, their treatment of me tended to be rather cool. But to give them credit, it was always correct. I was never discriminated against in any way, and in terms of travel opportunities and other facilities I was treated in just the same way as my colleagues.

Stories like Ssu Ching and the Great Painting Hoax are rare events in the life of any correspondent in Peking. Even so, there is no need for the correspondent to rely entirely for his stories on Hsinhua and the newspapers. He can travel inside China without much trouble—to an extent and with results that are often not appreciated by skeptics in the outside world.

Not everywhere, of course. Vast areas of China are ruled out for all but the most favored foreigners. It is many years since a Western correspondent has visited Sinkiang, the huge northwestern region where the Chinese have accused the Russians of fomenting trouble among the minority races. It is also a long time since correspondents have been to Lanchow in Kansu or Paotow in Inner Mongolia, probably because both are important sites for China's nuclear program. Journalists are also barred from Dairen and Port Arthur in former Manchuria and Hainan Island near Vietnam, almost certainly for reasons of security.

We never can be sure of the exact reasons, for the Chinese do their best to avoid giving a straight and simple refusal. We are usually told that our requested visit "is not convenient." This was the reply when the four Western correspondents applied to visit Tibet in September, 1965, for celebrations marking its long-delayed establishment as a so-called autonomous region. For weeks both Hsinhua and the Peking press had been swamping us with saccharine stories of happy emancipated serfs working side by side with their trusted Chinese "liberators" and singing paeans to Chairman Mao as they built a beautiful socialist future for themselves. It was all too good to be true, of course, especially since we had fairly solid evidence at that time of continued guerrilla activities by the Khampa tribesmen, as well as general resistance to Chinese schemes to set up agricultural cooperatives. Clearly, the Chinese could not afford to risk having an independent newsman pick up even the slightest evidence along these lines. Yet according to the Information Department, anonymous local officials in Lhasa had solemnly decided that a visit by the Western correspondents "would not be convenient at this time"—implying that it was all merely a matter of administrative arrangements. In this case, however, we made a news story of the refusal, drawing our own conclusions, which helped to put the propaganda in perspective.

Chinese officials would be pained if we accused them of hypocrisy. In fact, hypocrisy is a concept foreign to their traditional moral code. To them such circumlocutions are a form of the utmost courtesy and good manners—since nothing has been refused, no face has been lost on either side. On such occasions the Chinese use traditional tactics of the sort described by Lord Macartney, the first British Ambassador to China, as his embassy traveled by boat to Peking nearly two hundred years ago:

> The most refined politeness and sly good breeding appeared in the behaviour of all those Mandarins with whom we had any connection; but although we found an immediate acquiescence in words with everything we seemed to propose, yet, in fact, some ingenious pretence or plausible objection was usually invented to disappoint us. Thus when we desired to make little excursions from our boats into the towns, to visit any object that struck us as we went along, our wishes were seldom gratified. The refusal, or evasion, was, however, attended with so much profession, artifice and compliment that we soon grew reconciled and even amused with it.

With the same utmost courtesy the Chinese have a way of making the foreigner feel almost constantly guilty, or at least extremely apologetic, when it comes to putting forward his requests. I could never decide whether this was conscious or unconscious on their part. Either way, it seems to result from the apparently effortless sense of superiority that they convey. It is an invidious tactic, for unless the foreigner takes great pains to exert himself and his requests strongly, he begins to accept Chinese standards of how things are done, and falls into a state of passive acquiescence.

Although I collected a number of such evasive refusals, I did manage to travel fairly widely inside China, and not only to such obvious centers as Shanghai, Nanking, and Canton. Like many visiting journalists I was allowed to see something of the heavy industry in the northeast, formerly Manchuria, on a trip to Anshan, Shenyang, Changchun, and Harbin. On other occasions I traveled westward to Taiyuan, Sian, and Yenan, doubling back along the Yellow River to Loyang; to Kunming in the remote southwest (which was later closed to newsmen, probably because of the escalation in Vietnam), and to Tsinan, the seldom-visited capital of Shantung, China's second largest province.

However limited and supervised, such trips have great value in terms of any attempt to assess China's economic and social progress. It would be wrong to sum up China on the basis of observations made in Peking, for Peking is no more typical of China than New York City is of the United States. And in a country the size of China there are almost as many differences between Harbin in the cold northeast and Kunming in the semitropical southwest as there are between London and Rome. I also discovered in myself an interesting psychological reac-

tion. While in Peking, a correspondent tends to become
frustrated and cynical through dealing day after day with
all the noxious propaganda. When traveling, it is possible
to see real communes and real factories; and while one
often meets tiresome Party zealots, it is also possible to
encounter practical men tackling practical tasks who are
often refreshingly frank about their problems. When a
factory manager shows you some labor-saving device,
however gimcrack, designed by a worker on the spot, you
can better understand the pride and ingenuity that lie
behind all the dreary boasts of "self-reliance." When a
commune director shows you a reservoir and irrigation
ditches, built through the combined efforts of several
production brigades and sending water steadily to the rice
fields, you can better appreciate the practical side of these
giant farming units. Inevitably, I returned from these
trips with renewed sympathy for many of the aims and
aspirations of the Communist regime.

Wherever he goes, the correspondent is met and guided
by an interpreter from the China International Travel
Service and often by local or provincial government officials. At times the nomenclature is startling. Landing at
Taiyuan airport, I was approached as I left the plane by
two sturdy officials, bulkily encased in their blue cotton-
padded winter greatcoats. One, who turned out on close
inspection to be a woman, introduced herself as my interpreter. "And this," she said, turning to the other, "is Mr.
Nu, your principal host in Taiyuan. Mr. Nu is head of the
Shansi Province Department of Intercourse." At first, until
I realized what she really meant, it seemed that the
Chinese had finally organized sex to a truly Orwellian
degree. For the next three days the two officials were my
constant companions, and the lady prefaced her interpre-
tations of Mr. Nu's remarks with the ringing declaration:
"Our Chief of Intercourse says . . ." She must have
thought me feeble-witted, since I was always laughing,

but I never had the courage to tell this likeable lady that "Protocol" might be a more suitable translation.

On such trips the correspondent sees the best of factories and communes. This is hardly a sinister subterfuge, for it would be unnatural to expect any nation to show a visitor its less impressive aspects. And any correspondent who has done his homework can put his impressions into some sort of perspective. When he tours a commune that is fully irrigated and electrified, has several tractors and ample supplies of chemical fertilizer, he can describe it as well above average, but as an indication of the best that communes can achieve and what is eventually intended for the whole country. And even the best can often be revealing. When the director of a model commune states, as proof of rising living standards, that every family now has a quilt and a thermos flask, and that one in three has a bicycle, it is a good indication of how much poverty still remains. In former Manchuria, still the heartland of Chinese heavy industry, I was proudly shown giant complexes making steel, trucks, heavy machinery, machine tools, ball bearings, and all the other manifests of industrial progress. But in each factory, to varying degrees, there was obvious waste and inefficiency, and present output was clearly short of designed capacity. Better than all the cautious official statements, this trip showed me just how far China still lags behind the advanced economies of Japan and the Western world.

These trips allow the correspondent to assess living standards and the quality of daily life, and to conclude that in terms of food, clothing, housing, and basic consumer goods, other cities are almost as well supplied as Peking and Shanghai or suffer from the same shortages. Of course, we can only speak of the cities we are allowed to visit. But once on the spot, a correspondent is allowed to wander fairly freely and sometimes even encouraged to seek his own way around the back streets and to enter any

home of his choosing. Nor, in this well-drilled society, is
there much need to supervise all his movements. Often,
on these trips, I slipped out of my hotel for a solitary
stroll, and only once was I most definitely and conspicuously followed—this was during a stopover, on a bus ride
from Yenan to Sian, at Tungchuan, a grim industrial city
in Shensi Province which rarely sees a foreign guest. In
this case I could not be sure whether it was an official job
or the amateur effort of a zealous cadre. But after ninety
minutes of wandering through the muddy streets, I was
glad of my tail, since I was hopelessly lost. Time was
running out and the bus was about to leave, when he
politely tapped me on the shoulder and gently led me
back.

When he visits a factory, commune, or other institution,
the correspondent is involved in an intricate and strangely
formal ritual. He is seated under portraits of the Chinese
leaders (and sometimes those of Marx, Engels, Lenin, and
Stalin), offered a cigarette from a lacquered box, and the
first of endless cups of green Chinese tea (whatever my
time in China did to my liver, it certainly increased the
capacity of my bladder). Aside from the interpreter there
are almost always two Chinese officials present (any Chinese must be very sure of himself and his position to take
an interview on his own, and this rarely happens). Their
titles are usually ambiguous—something like Director of
the General Office. It is soon evident that one is the
practical man and the other the Party man. The Party
man usually shows less warmth, is shaky on technical
matters, and handles all the difficult political questions.
Almost always there is a secretary taking notes of everything that is said.

Then comes a "brief introduction," which lasts for anything from ten minutes to an hour. Usually consulting
notes, but sometimes reading verbatim from a scribbled
text, one of the officials will give a potted history of the

institution, stressing its steady progress "under the correct leadership of the Communist Party and Chairman Mao." Much attention is paid to the wicked practices and miserable conditions of pre-Communist days, and a correspondent's notebook becomes studded with the symbols *BL* and *AL*—Before and After Liberation. With luck, a few useful facts or figures may emerge from all this, including one or two dates, numbers of personnel, and perhaps an average wage. But almost always, especially at factories, production is described in terms of percentages, with a notable lack of any absolute or meaningful figures. The Chinese have released almost no economic statistics since 1959, when their economy was floundering amid the setbacks of the Great Leap Forward.

Then, as his tea cup is refilled for the seventh time, the correspondent is free to ask questions—an endeavor that is usually futile and often farcical. Sometimes he can emerge with a few genuinely useful facts and opinions (in a Soviet-equipped factory, for instance, they are always willing to speak about the perfidy of the Russians in 1960, when they suspended aid and withdrew their experts). But it is extremely difficult to have a factory official tell you in concrete terms how much his plant is actually producing. Some will make the astonishing assertion that they have no idea, others will maintain that the figures are unclear or incomplete. If told that this gives a poor impression of their managerial efficiency, some will reluctantly admit that production figures are a state secret. Usually the correspondent is left to make his own estimate on the basis of the subsequent tour of several workshops.

I think that, in general, the Chinese like to avoid a direct lie—although I have caught them out in one or two—and much prefer to be evasive. But on the rare occasion when a useful statistic is offered, it is best to be suspicious. In China's largest truck factory, at Changchun, I was told that actual current production was eighty trucks a day. Later, I learned that one week earlier a visiting delegation had been given an equally firm current-production figure of a hundred and twenty trucks a day. If everyone was telling the truth, the plant's production had dropped by 50 percent in seven days.

Often, too, the terms of reference are ambiguous. On a rice commune, for example, a figure for the average yield can relate to one or two or even three crops, and unless he is careful, the correspondent can be badly misled. Sometimes an unwary reporter can be led astray by the innocent inefficiency of a well-meaning interpreter. Much confusion is created by the Chinese habit of measuring in units of ten thousand, so that in the interpretation a zero is often dropped or added by mistake. In general, I learned to distrust figures and to rely largely on the evidence of my eyes.

Despite their reputation for subtle cunning, the Chinese can be awkwardly embarrassed by certain questions. Driving to a commune outside Tsinan, we passed a most impressive and rather sinister-looking factory, surrounded by a brick wall topped with barbed wire and searchlights, and with armed guards at the gates. "What do they make there?" I asked as casually as possible. There ensued a rapid flurry of Chinese between my interpreter and the local guide which seemed to last for several minutes. At last my interpreter turned to me. "It is not clear," he said simply.

Another time, on the outskirts of Kunming, we drove past an extremely large factory that covered many acres. Judging by the smokeless chimneys and the general lack of any activity, it seemed to be a major victim of the Great Leap Forward. When I asked my guide what was made there, he said he didn't know. When I asked him to stop the car and inquire, it was like hitting him below the belt. Distinctly embarrassed, he complied. After a brief conversation with the soldier at the gate, he reported that they had refused to tell him what they made inside. With that I threw a small, deliberate tantrum, and demanded that he convey my formal inquiry to his superiors. Eventually I received my answer: the factory turned out heavy machinery. But this information was delivered as I was taking a taxi to the airport—much too late to request a tour, as was clearly intended.

Such absurd little incidents are the frequent lot of the traveling correspondent in China. Sometimes they may simply indicate a passion for secrecy and a natural suspicion of prying foreigners. But as long as they occur, the wise correspondent remains skeptical of the more enthusiastic official claims.

2

The Pleasures
of Peking

High above Tien An Men Square in the center of Peking dragons and butterflies soared gracefully against an azure sky. Red and green, black and orange, they dipped their wings and tossed their delicate tails in the random gusts of a wintry wind. On the vast pavement far below, young boys worked the strings with grave concern, while their smaller brothers and sisters pranced and prattled with delight. Snug in their blue padded jackets, parents looked on with indulgent pride.

This was Spring Festival, the lunar holiday known to the outside world as Chinese New Year. Young and old, the Chinese were taking a three-day break from work and study. Traditionally, it was always a time to have a bath and a haircut, wear new clothes, engage in feasts, give gifts, and frighten devils with spluttering strings of firecrackers.

Until recently, virtually all Peking thronged to a single street fair in Lu Li Chang, the narrow thoroughfare of tiny cluttered shops just south of the city wall, where artisans through the centuries sold delicate jade and ivory carvings, paper-thin porcelain vases, and exquisite painted scrolls. Old China hands say it was a scrambling, grubby, and tumultuous event, with the Chinese seeming to relish their tumbled togetherness, finding sheer joy in their noisy scrape with suffocation.

Then the fair in Lu Li Chang was broken up and scattered throughout the capital. It was all very rational —as any city planner would agree—but something was lost.

Not far from the Square, along the vast Boulevard of Eternal Peace, more children thronged around some flimsy stalls. They did their best with the meager offerings—stuffing themselves with dumplings and toffee apples and delighting in the pinwheels and other cheap but clever wooden toys. But for all their capacity to make enjoyment out of minimal means, something seemed to be missing. Perhaps it was any sense of spontaneity, for it was all strangely subdued and even tame, this celebration of the premier Chinese holiday. As they roamed along the Boulevard the crowds seemed more dutiful than delighted. It could have been that my impressions were too subjective, but I could not help thinking that Spring Festival in Peking was lacking in festivity.

In all fairness, there was little room for indulgence. This was 1965, and after three relatively good harvests China had only just recovered from the setbacks and shortages of 1959–61, when a combination of bad weather and bungled planning had brought the nation to the brink of disaster. On trips around the country—from Harbin in the extreme northeast to Kunming in the far southwest—I had seen striking evidence of the comeback. But I had also been impressed by the enormity of the tasks that lay ahead.

On the giant farming communes Communist Party control is now less despotic and planning is more rational. Smaller production teams, usually a single village, are now the "basic accounting unit" and have some autonomy. No longer driven to make crude steel in backyard furnaces, peasants are once again allowed to tend their tiny private plots and to raise their private livestock.

These incentives have boosted farm yields, as have improved irrigation works and greater supplies of chemical fertilizers.

Of course, the dozen or so communes that I visited (out of seventy-four thousand) were clearly above average. Most were near major cities and seemed favored in terms of irrigation works, tractors, electrification, and fertilizer supplies. But on these communes, at any rate, the peasants looked healthy and well-fed, and there seemed to be new security from the ancient menace of droughts and floods. Yet when managers measured the progress of their commune in terms of rubber-tired carts, the fundamental poverty of the countryside was painfully apparent.

On visits to scores of factories I also saw the progress and the problems. It was not so much the giant blast furnaces and heavy machinery plants of the northeast that impressed me, for there, in former Manchuria, the Chinese were building on a Japanese base, and often with massive Soviet aid. It was more exciting and significant to visit the cities of the interior—Taiyuan, Sian, Loyang, Kunming—where the Chinese started almost from scratch (in some cases with Soviet aid, in others without) and steadily turned stagnant backwaters into bustling industrial centers.

Everywhere I found a new pragmatism and sense of sobriety. On the eve of the much-delayed Third Five Year Plan (which finally started in 1966) there was no tendency to repeat the wild slogans of the Great Leap Forward, when it was stated that China would overtake Britain in steel production in fifteen years. Instead, factory managers spoke prudently of expansion, preferring to stress the need for thrift and the raising of standards. Proudly they showed me their "technical innovations," which were often only flimsy contrivances, and boasted of "self-reliance," making a virtue of the necessity forced upon them by the abrupt ending of Soviet assistance.

It was clear that through their own sweat and ingenuity the Chinese had largely recovered from the drastic dislocations caused by a combination of the Soviet withdrawal, the "natural calamities," and their earlier euphoric planning. In such key areas as steel, transport, and chemicals, there were signs of definite expansion, yet many of the factories selected for foreign gaze were operating well short of capacity. After reading about the frantic bustle of the Great Leap Forward period, when it seemed that much of the nation was driven to exhaustion, I was struck by the leisurely pace of industrial life. In workshop after workshop I saw idle machines and idle men; with some notable exceptions the atmosphere in many factories was lethargic.

Later, however, there were ominous signs that the Chinese leaders were tempted to make at least a partial return to the sweeping, mass-line policies of the Great Leap Forward period. With the purge of so-called revisionists in the spring and summer of 1966, control of the nation seemed to rest with such dogmatists as Teng Hsiao-ping, the tough Secretary-General of the Chinese Communist Party. There was open talk of a "new leap" and some hints that the Party was itching to take back the peasants' private plots—a move that would undoubtedly be disastrous in terms of food supplies and morale in the countryside. At any rate, the increased preoccupation with political rectitude seemed bound to hinder the nation's economic development.

In the cities this slow progress and steady improvement were reflected in the daily life of the people. In Peking and other major cities the food supply was adequate, if hardly sumptuous. On all my trips I went early in the morning to the markets and watched the housewives swarming around the stalls and filling their baskets. Even in winter they were able to find fruit and vegetables at prices well within their budgets. Eggs and sugar were also plentiful and relatively cheap. To bring beef or pork to their tables was much more costly but far from impossible. Rice and wheat flour were still rationed but the allotments seemed more than stringent. Department-store counters were stocked with ever more varieties of consumer goods, and if a bicycle or a wristwatch could still take two months' wages, basic household goods were reasonably cheap, and there was even some small business in cameras and other luxury items.

Clothing was still the biggest problem, and many of the people were decidedly shabby, if not exactly ragged. Synthetic fibers had been introduced, but pawing her way through the counters, the cotton-conscious housewife still seemed suspicious of the new fabrics, which were also more expensive. And although the cotton-cloth ration had been increased, she still had to tend and patch her family's clothes with great care, since the average yearly ration was still little more than enough to make one high-collared jacket and a pair of trousers.

Still, there was a definite air of bustle in all the shops and markets—a marked contrast to the bad years, and showing the extent of China's comeback.

Watching over this steady recovery, the Chinese leaders were in a cautious mood. Proclaimed in newspapers and at political meetings for several weeks before, their Spring Festival directives to the people reflected their awareness that the recovery was still tentative. Just as important, they showed the Communists' determination to eradicate all old-fashioned superstitions and to impose upon the people their own cherished brand of puritanical and revolutionary zeal.

For Spring Festival, some things were OUT and others IN. OUT were lavish feasts and expensive presents, new clothing, the worshiping of ancestors and household gods, scrolls advocating prosperity and other material blessings, and calendars and New Year pictures showing emperors, courtesans, and other traditional subjects. IN were humble dinners, simple presents for children, and "revolution-ary" calendars portraying Chairman Mao Tse-tung or fat-cheeked peasants and beaming factory workers bulging with muscle and high endeavor (it is an interesting change that in classic Chinese painting, man is often a tiny figure, dwarfed by the majestic forms of nature; today, he appears on the paintings and posters as larger than life, dominating all).

Good deeds were in the air. The police were having a Love the People month, and everyone was exhorted to sing revolutionary songs, tell revolutionary tales, and help his neighbor. Collecting night soil was especially IN, and even a Vice-Mayor of Peking had been interviewed and photographed in the act, smiling sturdily.

Read outside the country, such directives give the im-pression that China is a gray, somber, humorless place, with ruthless rulers sternly bent on prohibiting even the simplest pleasures. Old China-hands shake their heads and bemoan the passing of the land they knew: dirty, corrupt, inefficient, and desperately poor—all that is granted—but also infused with life and color, with humor and dignity and a unique determination to find mirth and pleasure amid the most horrendous predicaments.

As seen from the inside the situation is rather more complex than outsiders imagine. Spring Festival may be somber and restricted, and simple pleasures viewed with some suspicion. But not all pleasures are banned, and Communist Party control is not as thorough as is often claimed. Above all, the children sucking their toffee apples and flying their lovely, intricate kites on Tien An Men Square still manifest the unique Chinese ability to derive great joy from the most humble occurrences.

It is the same throughout the year. In mid-winter the lake at the Summer Palace freezes up, and in the heart of the city there is ice on the Pei Hai (North Lake) and on the moat beneath the vermillion walls of the old Imperial City. According to Marco Polo, Kublai Khan had skating parties, and at the turn of the century the Manchu scholar Tun Li-chen found on the Pei Hai "skillful adepts, who skate like a dragonfly brushing the water, or a swallow piercing the waves." Today the parks and lakes are no longer the private preserve of the emperor and his court, and thousands of Pekinese enjoy their skating. Some, indeed, are like swallows or dragonflies, spurting with casual arrogance through the midst of the beginners, who stagger and stumble behind chairs which they rent for less than five cents and which save them from total disaster. You can see whole families skating hand-in-hand, and almost always there are young girl soldiers in floppy khaki uniforms, with pigtails, apple cheeks, and pretty smiles (for some reason, most of the really lovely girls I saw in China were in the army). Parts of the lakes are boarded off for hockey, played scrappily but with great enthusiasm. Foreigners join the skating and it hardly matters that the music over the loudspeakers is not "The Blue Danube" but "Socialism Is Good."

In spring and summer factories and offices organize excursions to the Summer Palace, the temples in the Western Hills, the Ming Tombs, and the Great Wall. On Sundays the roads out of the city are jammed with trucks and buses packed with workers, and as it snakes its way over hill and valley, the Great Wall is swarming with humanity. Even ancient grannies join the throng, hobbling painfully up the steep incline on their tiny bound feet. On top many of the workers sit in the sun, playing cards with raucous enthusiasm—while gambling is banned, and no money is ever *seen* to change hands, it is officially and solemnly stated that people playing cards are not necessarily manifesting a bourgeois ideology.

As they saunter around the sights many Chinese have transistor radios in the cheap plastic handbags which

everyone—men and women alike—seems to carry. As
they view the ancient monuments it is often to the raucous, jangled strains of Chinese opera. Some have cameras, still expensive, but already something of a status
symbol. With elaborate care young men pose their girl
friends in stiff, self-conscious attitudes beside stone lions
and temple gates. In the Western Hills the green slopes
are speckled with huge red banners carried by columns of
children on hikes.

In the city itself enjoyment can be had with less exer-
tion. Through the long summer evenings many Pekinese
flock to a Sinkiang restaurant in the western suburbs
which has tables in the open air and serves watermelon,
beer, and juicy mutton slabs on skewers. Here there are
dating couples as well as groups of stern-faced Party
members taking their supper after some late meeting.
During the day old men with wise and wizened faces
wheel their grandchildren to the parks in bamboo carriages. While the children clamber around the swings and
slides, the old men, surrounded by intent spectators of all
ages, play Chinese chess with their cronies on rough stone
benches. In the park near my hotel there were always
Chinese men (but never women) on the tennis court.
Immaculately dressed in long white flannels, they played
an old-fashioned, baseline game with much grace and
absolute decorum. On the field nearby there was often
noisier activity, with swarms of boys playing basketball
and soccer.

Life goes on—much as it always has—but to find it, you
have to go behind the great boulevards and the new
public buildings. For these have a pompous air that seems
remote from the relaxed and lively spirit of Peking. To
their credit, the Communists have retained and restored
the great gates and palaces, the temples and pagodas
which make Peking for me, as it was for Marco Polo, the

most fabulous city in the world. Only the wall around the old Tartar City is being steadily demolished, but this is probably a practical necessity.

It was not enough for the Communists to restore the old. Understandably, they shared the feelings of Kublai Khan, who, on moving his capital to Peking, decreed that beautiful and imposing palaces be built, in order to command the respect of the Empire. And so they have put up their own monuments, but with less success than the great Khan.

Completing the square around majestic Tien An Men (the Gate of Heavenly Peace), the Great Hall of the People and the giant museum are heavy and grandiose. While Chinese architects have never been afraid of huge blocks, broad walls, and clear lines, these new creations seem too solemn and pretentious, with little sense of grace. The same is true of the airport building, the railway station, the new hotels and exhibition halls—each an uneasy compromise between traditional forms and the demands of a new dynasty determined to manifest its own solemn sense of socialist grandeur. Perhaps the problem was insoluble, but future generations of Pekinese may well bemoan the fact that the architects were allowed to show only such a scanty imagination.

The new housing is even worse. To meet a definite need the Chinese are steadily building blocks of apartments, especially in the suburbs. However cramped, with whole families compressed into two or three tiny rooms, these offer thousands of Pekinese more space and facilities than they have had ever before, and at very low rents which are usually only about 5 percent of a workingman's salary. But they are outright monstrosities: grim, drab slabs of red brick or yellow stucco set in stolid rows, without any sense that these are homes, places where people live. Aside from offering a perpetual insult to their inhabitants, these ugly blocks are a slur on the beauty of Peking. Apart from their hideous design, most seem poorly built of cheap materials, and many are already crumbling and peeling into slums. Only in Shanghai, always a pacesetter, have I seen new housing that is something less than totally offensive to the eye. There, in satellite towns, apartment blocks are better built, show less monotony in design, and are often pleasantly set off by trees and grass.

Really to know Peking, to sense the rhythm of its daily life, you have to leave the bigger boulevards for the hutungs—the narrow residential alleys that give the capital so much of its character. Drab and dusty, they form vast labyrinths between the larger streets. In the center, around the Imperial City, some are paved, and even wide enough for cars. Along such hutungs, you find the gray stone walls and brilliant red doors that hide some of the larger Chinese homes, with their intricate courtyards and corridors. You also find some embassies and government offices (the Chinese must be the only major power to have their Foreign Ministry in an alley). But outside the wall, in what foreigners once called the Chinese City, life along the hutungs is poor and primitive. The houses are small shacks, often desperately propped up with poles and scaffolding. Inside they are dark and crowded, and on the hot summer days the people come out in the open to seek fresh air, making the hutungs crowded and clamorous. Often stripped to the waist, old men and women sit on stools, fanning themselves and swapping tales and gossip, while naked and grubby children play noisy games around their feet. There is dirt and great hardship, and I sometimes saw tattered old men rooting determinedly through piles of garbage. But there are few obvious signs of undernourishment or disease, and there is great bustle and a sense of life being lived with much good-humored fortitude.

In the afternoons I sometimes went to Tien Chiao, a crowded, dirty complex of shops and theaters outside the city wall. Tien Chiao means Bridge of Heaven; there is no bridge today, but the bazaar and fair have survived the fall of dynasties, the Japanese occupation, and the Communist victory. This is where, for centuries, the country folk have come to sell their produce, to do their shopping, and to be entertained at cut-rate prices.

There is nothing fancy about Tien Chiao. Children, watched over by their gossiping grannies, run happily and often naked through the alleys. A wandering barber sets down his stool whenever he finds a customer and draws a curious crowd as he administers a vigorous shampoo. There are small shops, food stalls, and a one-room factory where cotton sandals are made. You can sit at a rough wooden table and, for a few cents, have a pot of tea and a long sticky roll. For not much more you can have your picture taken, riding a cardboard motorcycle before a cardboard Forbidden City.

And here, above all, are the entertainers—in the open air, under a canvas roof, or inside a tiny theater—for Tien Chiao is the home of folk art in the Chinese capital. In one small shack wrestlers with splendid bulging bellies grunt and grapple on an earthen floor, taking their cleverly contrived falls with shouts of mock anguish. Along another alley sixteen lithe acrobats simultaneously ride the same bicycle round and round a narrow stage. Outside another theater a barker harangues the crowd, while inside a woman storyteller relates a complicated tale of passion and adventure with singsong cadences and a wealth of subtle gestures. In an open space a magician with a comic patter exhorts onlookers to throw their pennies and enthralls the wide-eyed children with skillful sleight-of-hand.

Although the setting is far from lavish, there is no lack of artistry and dedication. Performers from Tien Chiao have been sent abroad on an official tour. Peking Operas are played here on dingy stages, but with all the traditional rich costuming, heavy makeup, elaborate tumbling, and stylized gestures. Tien Chiao is as timeless a part of Peking as the temples and pagodas, and much more lively. For me it was always a welcome break, and the tedious propaganda and endless Party campaigns seemed far away. I liked to think that the Chinese felt the same, and, judging by their laughter and high spirits, I suspect they did.

Yet nothing in China is ever really remote from politics. While the Chinese leaders do not prohibit simple pleasures, they try to make them serve their own political ends. Excursion parties to the palaces and pagodas hear potted lectures on the iniquities of the old order. Hiking and swimming are advocated as "military sports," and young people are told to toughen their sinews so they can better defend their country against any invader, especially the United States. While old men still wheel their grandchildren in the parks, and the three-generation family unit remains more or less intact, the leaders regard the family unit with great distrust since, with its traditional place at the heart of Chinese society, it threatens the authority of a regime which demands total allegiance and tolerates no rival. Cutting through centuries of Confucian tradition, Party zealots tell the youth that their basic loyalty must be to the state rather than their elders.

Even the simple pastime of sitting on the stoop and telling tales is under attack. With its usual lack of humor the Peking *People's Daily* described the "summer evening chatting ground" as a battlefield of fierce ideological struggle. Along the hutungs, it stated, some people were telling revolutionary stories and singing revolutionary songs. But others "are talking a great deal about food, clothing, and having a good time, and telling superstitious and feudal stories." Unless challenged by vigilant Communist Party officials, so-called bourgeois elements might use the summer-evening chatting ground to spread their doctrines and prepare for counter-revolution. And it is the same in the teahouses where, the *People's Daily* warned, the same bad elements were actively at work.

Even Tien Chiao is suffering a decline. It is still cited in the official guidebook—one of the most dreary of its kind—with a predictable political gloss: in pre-Communist days Tien Chiao was a chaotic place where gangsters, bullies, swindlers, and spies ran riot; today the working-people have stood on their own feet, and the criminal elements are suppressed. But old hands say that the squeeze is on, that the color and vitality of Tien Chiao are being steadily drained away, and that each year finds fewer theaters and sideshows. And in Tien Chiao, as in the more formal theaters, the old operas and stories are being steadily replaced by ones with "revolutionary" themes.

As a newcomer to China, I had been startled, perhaps naïvely so, to find the people so relaxed and so natural in their everyday life. I knew already that for most Chinese life was better than under any previous regime—that food supplies, although hardly lavish, were distributed fairly, that tremendous progress had been made in health and hygiene, that vicious exploitation by landlords and factory owners had been eliminated, and that the shameful foreign concessions were no more. I knew that whatever the cost in terms of totalitarian suppression, most Chinese had a better chance to lead their lives with security and even some dignity. But after more than a year of reading Chinese propaganda from the outside, I was also very much aware of the rigid political doctrines and the ceaseless political campaigns. From the outside I wondered whether any Chinese had any time to call his own, and whether it was ever possible to relax.

The reality is much more complex than I had imagined.

It is wildly wrong to describe China as a grim wasteland, where people are herded from one campaign to another and simple joys are savagely suppressed. It is equally false to assert that Communism has made no impact, and that the "traditional" Chinese—cunning and conservative, patient and slyly humorous—is quietly biding his time and preserving his values intact despite the demands of yet another despotic dynasty. For while much remains the same, much has been changed.

Gliding high over Tien An Men Square, those delicate kites reflect a love of beauty and a capacity for pleasure that have far from withered away after seventeen years of Communist rule. But for the boys who fly them there is a new society that makes demands and offers opportunities undreamed of by their parents.

3

Envoys
to the
Great Within

On the sea, east of Peking, is a small town called Pie Tai Ho, with a beach and a hotel. Here, in July and August, foreign residents in Peking are permitted to take their holidays. There is little to do except sleep and lie in the sun. But even when engaged in such innocent pursuits, foreigners arouse the stern suspicion of Chinese officials and are subject to careful regulation.

There is a notice board on the beach with instructions in Chinese, Russian, and English. Some of the points are routine, but three are remarkable:

—Sea bathers must wear dark-colored swimming suits.

—The mentally defective should be kept from sea bathing.

—To promote the spirit of friendship and mutual help, collective sea bathing is recommended.

(signed) *The People's Council of Pei Tai Ho District.*

One pictures them, the good People's Representatives of Pei Tai Ho, sitting around their council table late into the night, drinking endless cups of tea and cleverly contriving their regulations in order to avoid that most dreaded prospect: a *mad* diplomat, wearing *white* trunks, charging down the beach, determined to swim *all by himself.*

It was only in 1861 that the Chinese established their Foreign Ministry. Before that they made do with an Office for Barbarian Affairs. Today something of the arrogance implied in that earlier title is still manifest in Chinese dealings with foreign residents and visitors. For while it would be absurd to maintain that Communism has not brought great changes to China and has not influenced the mentality and methods of the leaders, the Chinese name for their country is still Chung Kuo—the Middle Kingdom. As under previous dynasties, the Chinese still show deep feelings of cultural and racial superiority, and a conviction that the world revolves around Peking. To them, to some extent, we are still barbarians who come bearing tribute to the Celestial Court and are graciously permitted in turn to study the excellence of Chinese civilization.

Today nearly fifty nations have embassies or trading offices in Peking, with hundreds of diplomats, secretaries, and family members. About thirty foreign correspondents are resident in the capital, and there are also several hundred foreign students, language teachers, and other experts. Then there are the visitors: businessmen, delegations from friendly countries, and even, to an increasing extent, tourists.

The size of this influx would have scandalized officials of earlier dynasties. After the arrival of Marco Polo and the early Jesuit travelers, the Mandarins worked desperately to keep the foreigners away from Peking. In the last decade of the eighteenth century, the British envoy, Lord Macartney, received a polite but firm rebuff, and was told that there was no question of nations establishing embassies in Peking. To his sovereign, George III, Macartney brought back the famous edict of the great Emperor Ch'ien Lung, which said in part: "As to what you have requested in your message, O King, namely to be allowed to send one of your subjects to reside in the Celestial Empire to look after your Country's trade, this does not conform to the Celestial Empire's ceremonial system, and definitely cannot be done. . . ." When the opium trade and other commercial prospects led the European powers to force their way into China in the nineteenth century, Chinese officials tried to limit their incursions to Canton and other southern ports. It was only in the last decades of the century, after Chinese forces had suffered shattering defeats at the hands of the marauding and avaricious Europeans, that the foreigners began to establish their missions in Peking.

Communist rule has made significant changes in this traditional antipathy toward foreign incursions. Seeking leadership of both the Communist and Afro–Asian worlds, the Chinese welcome their envoys and embassies. Trying to outflank the United States, and needing their own outposts abroad, the Chinese tolerate the missions of those Western countries, such as Britain, with whom political differences are often acute. In the wake of the dispute with Moscow, Peking proclaims a proud policy of self-reliance while actually turning to the Western world and Japan for the goods and equipment which its nascent industry demands. Times have changed since Ch'ien Lung told George III: "We have never valued ingenious articles, nor do we have the slightest need of your country's manufactures. . . ." Today such "ingenious articles" as fertilizer plants and chemical works are very much in demand, and the presence in Peking of their salesmen must be tolerated. Foreigners are also being hired as language teachers, since China's growing ties with the outside world create a demand for ever more interpreters. Even tourists have their place, since they bring valuable foreign exchange and on carefully limited tours they can be impressed by China's undoubted social and economic progress.

But the *attitude* of the Chinese to the foreigner has hardly changed, and their *methods* of handling him are strikingly similar to those of previous dynasties. It was all summed up a century ago by the Emperor Hsien-feng:

> Everything must be handled calmly. Do not entertain their requests. If you take special pains to control them rigidly and check them courteously, how far will these barbarians' cunning get them?

There is no doubt about the courtesy. It is evident from the start at Shum Chun, on the border with Hong Kong, where customs officials speaking excellent English are polite and considerate to a degree that can only astonish anyone who has dealt with their counterparts in other countries. This first impression is confirmed all along the line, with interpreters, guides, waiters, airline steward-esses, and even taxi drivers going out of their way to be agreeable. Wherever he travels the foreigner is offered the very best in food and accommodation—in fact, he is not permitted to venture anywhere where the best is not available.

Sometimes courtesy is carried to an embarrassing ex-tent. Boarding a crowded bus in Canton, I heard the girl conductor bark an order. Half the passengers immediately stood up to offer me their seats—including three old men, some young soldiers of the People's Liberation Army, and a lady who must have been in her eighth month of pregnancy. As we arrived late one evening at a theater in Taiyuan, the capital of Shansi province, my interpreter marched me boldly down the aisle to the front row, where he brusquely turfed two ancient grannies out of the best seats. As they hobbled painfully away on their canes and bound feet, I made a strong protest, but it did no good— foreigners in China get the best treatment, and that is that.

For the Chinese there is an important distinction. In the old days, they say, the foreign powers forced themselves upon a China that was weak and corrupt, seizing and maintaining special privileges through the power of their troops and gunboats. Today a strong and sovereign China offers these privileges freely, as proof of independence and innate good manners. Before there was subservience; now there is pride.

Such, at any rate, is the official explanation. It is hard to know what the people really think. On the one hand they are told that every foreigner in China is an honored guest of the government and the people. On the other they are instructed every day, through all the propaganda media, in the iniquitous history of the white man in China and in the present depravity of his "imperialist" or "revisionist" system. This may lead to some confusion in the Chinese mind. At any rate, on rare occasions, stark hostility breaks through the veneer of courtesy.

Traveling by train from Canton to Peking, I alighted at a station and walked along the platform as my Chinese fellow travelers faithfully performed their morning exercises and flocked to food stalls burdened with hard-boiled eggs, fresh fruit, and long sticky rolls. I had a camera strung around my neck but had made no attempt to use it, when I was suddenly accosted by a young man with bristly hair and sunglasses who was clearly enraged by the mere sight of the instrument and suspected me of some dire intention. Planting himself before me and pointing at the camera, he launched a long harangue in harsh, uncompromising terms. A curious crowd gathered around us as he literally screamed at me for several minutes. It was a sordid, senseless little incident, but what I remember most is the naked hostility and even hatred in his eyes—hatred directed at myself as a representative of the white race which had ravaged China in the past and still sought to deny her a rightful place in the sun.

Such incidents are the exception and courtesy is much more common. But if good manners are a Chinese trait, so are a lively sense of the ridiculous and a ribald sense of humor. Walking through a Chinese crowd, a Chinese-speaking foreigner will often find that his personal appearance is the subject of much discussion. "Hairy One" and "Big Nose" are still directed at Europeans, and "Big Penis" is sometimes heard. One of the more endearing aspects of the Chinese is their capacity to be gently amused at the antics of all the barbarians.

Sometimes the foreigners cause perplexity and confusion, especially since we are now present in such diversity. On Hangchow's West Lake three young Englishmen had beached their boat to walk around one of the islands, leaving their shoes behind. One, who understood Chinese, overheard an old Chinese couple in anxious debate. Said the old man, "Yes, they *are* walking barefoot, but they don't look like Africans to me."

Few guides and interpreters show such curiosity. Sometimes I was questioned about conditions in Canada, but although my answers were modestly phrased, they were clearly not believed. For as any reader of the Chinese press can tell you, it is well known that in the Western world the masses live in great poverty and are greatly suppressed by a tiny ruling clique. At a state banquet in the Great Hall of the People an official of the Foreign Ministry who had studied in New York maintained that the worst East Side slums were typical of the whole nation, and stubbornly refused to acknowledge that many industrial workers in the United States had their own cars and homes. Some of my guides knew that Canada sold great amounts of wheat to China, although this has never been reported in the Chinese press. But when I stated that because of such sales, at least a few Prairie farmers drive Cadillacs and take their holidays in Florida, I was taken for a liar. A similar lack of comprehension was shown by an interpreter for a delegation of well-heeled Albertan farmers, who delighted his charges by constantly referring to them as "Canadian peasants."

Although disturbing, such reactions are understandable, and it would be cruel to mock the Chinese for failing to comprehend the great gap between their living standards and those in the West. Much more disturbing, however, is the general lack of curiosity among most guides, interpreters, and other Chinese with whom contact is allowed, especially when this is accompanied by smug assertions that China is in the forefront of all human progress. It is distressing and frightening to encounter minds that are so completely closed—either through fear of making some compromising statement or through innate feelings of superiority. And what can you say to the young guide who asks you, with great politeness, "And when will you have *your* revolution?"

As the Chinese open their gates to more foreigners, they are also perfecting their methods of isolating and controlling each resident and visitor. As Ch'ien Lung told George III:

> Moreover, the territories ruled by the Celestial Empire are vast, and for all the envoys of vassal states coming to the capital there are definite regulations regarding the provision of quarters and supplies to them and regarding their movements. There never has been any precedent for allowing them to suit their own convenience.

In the last century the first foreign traders reaching Canton were isolated in their factories on Shameen Island, carefully separated from the rest of the city and allowed to deal only with a few selected junior officials. Today foreign residents in Peking are being steadily pushed into a similar segregation.

Most of the language teachers and other foreign experts are housed far out in the western suburbs, behind guarded gates at the Druzbha, or Friendship Hostel. Built in happier days for the thousands of Soviet experts who flocked to Peking, this huge compound now has a funereal aspect. Whole wings are closed and in others teachers from Britain, France, and other European nations, as well as Africa and Latin America, lead cramped and isolated lives along the dark and dingy corridors.

Closer to the center of town many of the foreign embassies established in the last fifteen years are grouped around the Wai Chiao Ta Lou—the Big Building for Foreigners. This is a huge complex of apartments where hundreds of diplomats and secretaries and a few correspondents manage to live in reasonable comfort. Farther out to the east and halfway to the airport is an area called San Li Tun. Here are the newer embassies—those of France and the African nations—as well as more apartment blocks. Here, too, the Chinese keep on building more embassies, confident that other nations will soon follow the lead of France in extending diplomatic recognition to Peking.

A few of the more fortunate countries still keep embassies and homes in the heart of Peking. Many of these are along Legation Street, a narrow road of much atmosphere and charm just inside the southern city wall, lined with silk-flower trees and horsetail-flower trees. This was the heart of the old Legation Quarter, the privileged preserve of foreigners under the last emperors. Here, at the turn of the century, the foreigners lined the walls to fight off the ferocious Boxer rebels, who were egged on by the Empress Dowager in a last desperate attempt to drive out all the Barbarians, only to be defeated by an international relief force that sacked the Forbidden City and sent Old Buddha fleeing as far as Sian. Still resentful of these past humiliations, Chinese officials are slowly squeezing out the few remaining foreign missions; in a few years all will be in San Li Tun.

The same is true of the few embassies and private homes scattered in other parts of the capital. Along the narrow, clamorous hutungs a few lucky foreigners still live in Chinese houses, with their gray stone walls, bright red doors, and peaceful courtyards. To sit in such a courtyard on a summer evening, watching the moon above the willow trees, is to understand the charm that Peking held for residents in earlier decades. But from these houses, too, the foreigners are gradually being evicted. According to one report, Chen Yi, the Foreign Minister, has said it is imperative to remove all foreigners from the hutungs, since they give the local people "wrong ideas." After watching the curious crowds who gather outside an embassy or foreign home whenever there is a party or reception—gaping at our cars and clothes like so many movie fans at a premiere—I suspect he has a point. It is also rumored that eventually even the Wai Chiao Ta Lou will be taken over and that *all* the foreigners will then be living in remote and splendid isolation at San Li Tun.

It clearly suits the Chinese to have all the foreigners segregated in well-defined areas. This scheme has one great merit aside from its tidiness: it makes it more difficult for the foreigner to have any contact with the Chinese people. Officials spend much time preventing such contacts, partly to shield their people from the contamination of foreign ideas, partly to keep the foreigner from finding out too much about what is really happening around him. In this the Chinese follow the precepts of Chi Ying, an Imperial clansman who memorialized the Throne in 1844:

> Furthermore, the various barbarians have come to live at peace and in harmony with us. We must give them some sort of entertainment and cordial reception; but we are on guard against an intimate relationship in our intercourse with them.

And Chi Ying was considered by many of his colleagues to be something of a dangerous radical, much too friendly to the foreigners.

In Chi Ying's time foreign envoys to the Great Within were expected "to come and be transformed"—to be awed by the majesty of the Dragon Throne and to be impressed by the clear superiority of Chinese ways. Not until the last decades of the nineteenth century was there any thought that China might have anything to learn from the foreign powers; even then it was only Western military might that impressed most Chinese reformers. Convinced that their own culture was matchless, they wished to "use foreign ways to protect Chinese ideas."

There is a similar reluctance today to enter into any exchange of ideas with the foreigner. While the Chinese concede the West's great technological superiority and are willing to pay hard currency in order to acquire that technology's products, it is still affirmed that the Chinese political and social system is vastly more progressive than that of any other nation. Thus the function of the foreign envoy has changed little in Chinese eyes, and while he is permitted to study Chinese ways, the Chinese show scant interest in his own ideas and cultural background.

This pattern becomes evident when a diplomat meets Chinese officials, either at some social function or in a formal audience. Politely but firmly the diplomat is instructed in the Chinese position; however hard he may try there is no question of any meaningful discussion or dialogue. This is true even of nations which, like France, have established diplomatic relations in hopes of exerting some influence on the Chinese and of drawing them into the give-and-take of contemporary diplomacy. All such efforts are rebuffed.

In fact, the diplomat often finds he is much less important in Chinese eyes than are cultural groups, fellow-travelers, and even "true Marxist–Leninists" from his own country. These visitors are often accorded a lavish welcome in Peking and can meet senior leaders whom the poor diplomat has only viewed from a distance. As in the past, the Chinese favor those foreigners most disposed to acknowledge Chinese predominance rather than those who show signs of independence.

Yet the Chinese are not tied to their traditions. Indeed, vast areas of their culture have been ruthlessly set aside or drastically reinterpreted. Some of the Chinese methods of treating foreigners show as many parallels to those of other Communist countries as they do to those of the Ch'ing Dynasty. Diplomats who served in Stalinist Russia find many similarities in the way they are kept at arm's length in Peking. But the parallels to the treatment of Lord Macartney and his successors are so numerous that they indicate a deep psychological response to the foreigner that has altered very little.

As a rule the Chinese try to limit our contacts to servants, interpreters, and teachers of language and painting. In some cases this narrow circle is slightly enlarged to include Chinese married to foreigners, and a few others who have long-standing ties with the embassies. Only one doctor in Peking is allowed to visit foreign homes, and even tailors have recently been discouraged from making such visits. It is almost impossible for a Chinese to enter an embassy, foreign apartment building, or hotel on an unauthorized call, since police or other security men guard the doors.

Most of the authorized meetings take place in an embassy or foreign home, and—as part of the general tightening of restrictions on foreigners—these have become even more official and less social than before. I know a few Chinese who were once allowed to visit foreign homes for dinner or a game of bridge; lately, they have politely declined such invitations. Only rarely is a foreigner invited to a Chinese house. Except for the usual banalities in shops and restaurants, spontaneous conversations of any substance are rare—even when a foreigner speaks the language—since every Chinese knows that he is hardly ever out of the sight or hearing of some Party member or zealous activist.

There are exceptions, especially among the foreign teachers and students who have closer contact with young Chinese. It is more difficult for diplomats and correspondents, but not impossible. While shipping film in the post office one day, I was approached by an elderly Chinese who introduced himself in excellent English. For obvious reasons, I will state only that he was a professional man of some stature who had studied and worked in the West; he was obviously starved for contact with a foreigner. Somewhat to my dismay, he launched a loud and lengthy monologue, while other Chinese in the post office looked on with curious concern. Although critical of the Communists, he spoke with neither bitterness nor anger, and was apparently more amused by their follies. He was, I suspect, a man who had achieved a certain level of serenity or at least resignation.

He spoke mainly of the overwhelming Party control: "You can't go anywhere unless they let you. I'd like to travel abroad once more, but it's impossible to get an exit permit. I have a large house, but I'm no longer allowed to entertain foreigners. I can't visit you at your hotel—they have security men everywhere and they wouldn't let me in. I'm allowed to import technical books, but no newspapers or magazines.

"People come here [he mentioned two of the better known Western experts on China] and they see only what they're meant to see. No one is allowed to see the real poverty. The newspapers publish only what is good."

He laughed about the rationing. "Coupons—coupons for everything. And credentials." He opened his wallet and showed me how both sides were filled with different colored cards and coupons. No professional man earned more than 350 yuan (about $160) a month, he said, but it didn't matter, since there was nothing to spend it on.

"Still," he added, "you must give the devil his due. Just look at what they've done. Fantastic things! Public health, for instance, and getting rid of prostitutes. And they're honest. There's no corruption, no more squeeze of any sort. You have to give them credit—they *are* dedicated."

He shrugged his shoulders, shook my hand, and waved goodbye. At the door of the post office, he turned and shouted back: "Of course, you know we'll never meet again." Then he was gone.

Such a conversation is refreshing because it is so rare. Perhaps he felt secure in his old age and professional standing, perhaps he was past caring. Of the score of people who overheard his booming monologue, at least one probably knew some English, and even the others would have had good grounds for suspicion. Certainly he was taking a risk. I know from another very unhappy personal experience that Chinese who meet foreigners without official approval have a way of disappearing, however innocent the contact.

As for authorized contacts, these are almost always disappointing. With a few exceptions interpreters and teachers are very cautious in their conversation; after all, most have bourgeois backgrounds and are themselves under constant suspicion. Most, we assume, are obliged to make regular reports on the foreigners with whom they have contact. There is something very sad about these people. Because they have dealings with foreigners, they are permitted to abjure the standard sloppy trousers and high-collared Chung Shan tunic. The men often wear smart, Western-style business suits, and the women are allowed to appear in cheongsams, and with permanent waves and even jewelry. They are also relatively well-off, since a good interpreter earns nearly $100 a month, or at least three times the average factory wage. But while comparatively affluent, they seem spiritually impoverished, out of tune with their society, wasted, wistful, truncated. This, I should stress, is very much a subjective impression, since I was always very careful never to say anything which might embarrass or compromise these people, and they in turn were always very circumspect in their remarks to me.

Once, as a break from the dreary round of "revolutionary" plays and operas, I attended a performance at the Tien Chiao Theater of a French classical ballet troupe. At least three quarters of the audience were Chinese, and I knew that most had schemed for weeks to obtain their tickets. For them it was clearly a meaningful and nostalgic experience. Some wore European dress, others were clothed in Chinese garb as smartly as is still possible. There was something about their enthusiasm, their expressions, and their bearing that greatly moved me. Perhaps for the first time I was seeing a fair cross section of the sort of Chinese intellectuals with whom Westerners once had close contact. And seeing made me jealous, resentful, and even angry that such contacts should be broken and that the two cultures should now have so little meaningful communion.

Aside from isolating foreigners, the Chinese often seek to cut off groups of foreigners from each other. On the tours arranged for diplomats great efforts are made to keep the Europeans separated from their former colonial subjects, and the Chinese show some anguish whenever an "imperialist" sits down at a table with someone from the Afro–Asian world. Instinctive ties between white and colored members of the Commonwealth seem especially to infuriate the Chinese. In Peking foreign teachers at the Druzbha are subjected to ideological persuasion and are sternly warned against having any contacts with their own embassies, although this advice is cheerfully disregarded by many.

In trying to prevent the foreigner from finding out too much about local conditions, the Chinese often resort to ludicrous stratagems. They are especially concerned to keep local newspapers out of our hands. On several of my trips outside Peking my hosts contrived the most incredible excuses to explain why such newspapers were not available. On one diplomatic tour a Western diplomat purchased a local newspaper from a street vendor, only to have his guide tear it from his hands and have the vendor return the money. In the next city the same diplomat went with the same guide to a newsstand. He was allowed to buy Peking papers, but was flatly told that he couldn't buy the local ones, which were conspicuously on display. At this point the diplomat—who came from a country which has fairly cordial relations with Peking—made a strong and emphatic protest. By the following day the guide had clearly sought instructions from higher quarters, and in order to avoid an embarrassing incident, had been overruled. At the next station the diplomat was met on the platform by a vendor who headed straight for him and ostentatiously offered him a local newspaper, and during the rest of the tour the local papers were delivered to his hotel room.

In enforcing their prohibitions, the Chinese rarely resort to melodramatic methods. If the distinction can be made, China is not so much a police state as a Party state.

There is no need to follow foreigners in the street, since
the Party is such a ubiquitous presence, at least in the
cities. Surrounded by Chinese, the foreigner is highly
conspicuous, and any suspicious actions will almost certainly be noticed by some Party cadre or other loyal
citizen.

I have no firm proof that telephones are tapped and
rooms are bugged, although most residents assume that
they are and govern their conversations accordingly.
There is evidence that the Chinese read cables. Letters
seem to be opened on a selective basis—my own estimate
would be one in five; this is easy to judge, since the flaps
are resealed clumsily, and the backs of the envelopes are
often smeared with glue.

In all fairness, the Chinese have certain standards of
correct behavior and do not emulate the Russians in
fabricating incidents with foreigners; they also lack some
of the provocations, since there are no American diplomats in Peking, and other foreign military attachés do not
engage in the sort of spying that is common in the Soviet
Union. Immediately after the Communist victory in 1949
many foreign residents, including missionaries and businessmen, were jailed as spies. But in recent years, to the
best of my knowledge, there have been no trumped-up
incidents involving residents or visitors. Certain foreigners
have been told to leave the country, but in every such
case I know of, the Chinese had some grounds for action.

Confined and closely watched, cut off from the Chinese
all around him, the foreign resident in Peking leads a
strange, hermetic life. There is much solidarity in the face
of a common adversary—in spite of political differences,
Western "imperialists" and Communist "revisionists" entertain each other with considerable cordiality, and to an
extent that would probably not occur in any other major
capital. This, I am told, is a recent development resulting

mainly from the Sino–Soviet rift. In earlier years there were three distinct groups among the foreign community —Communists, Westerners, and neutralists—and very little overlapping. Today a Communist diplomat entertains his Western colleagues, and plays loud American pop music on a West German tape recorder in order to drown the conversation.

This intimacy can be embarrassing, since the foreign community is so small, our distractions are so limited, and there is an inordinate amount of gossip—everyone knows about everyone else's romance, sometimes before it has begun. It is also a distinct handicap that everyone knows everyone else's car, and where it should normally be parked.

Amusements are few and precious. Foreign residents, as mentioned earlier, can take an uneventful summer holiday at Pei Tai Ho, and it is also possible to drive to the port of Tientsin after giving forty-eight hours' notice to the Public Security Bureau. Any other trip requires permission from the Foreign Ministry, and more often than not officials will reply that such a trip is "not convenient." Unless he is lucky enough to be included on the semiannual diplomatic tour (which is usually limited to two persons from each embassy), the foreign resident in Peking does very little traveling.

Within Peking and its environs the foreigner is more or less free to roam as he likes, provided that he keeps inside the permitted twenty-mile radius. In autumn, when the maple trees turn a violent red and gold, it is pleasant to drive out of the city for picnics at the Ming Tombs or visits to the temples in the Western Hills. Skating in the winter and boating in the summer are other ways of escaping the claustrophobic atmosphere of the foreign quarters. In the evenings scores of restaurants can serve a sumptuous banquet—peppery Szechwan dishes, crisp Peking duck, elaborate Cantonese sweetmeats, or, in winter, slices of beef and mutton cooked Mongolian-style on open stoves. But night life as such hardly exists. It is virtually impossible for the foreigner to stomach the banal "revolutionary" themes of the movies, plays, and operas—however skillfully presented—and traditional Peking Opera is now only performed for brief periods around National Day and May Day.

There is, of course, the Saturday night dance at the International Club, an event of monumental hilarity. Formerly the Peking Club, an exclusive preserve for foreigners in the heart of the old Legation Quarter, this staid house is now run by the Chinese government. Each Saturday night a Chinese orchestra performs with earnest concentration in the main ballroom behind potted palms and under slowly revolving fans. Mostly they play waltzes and dance tunes from the 1920s, and it must be the only dance band anywhere that still uses a soprano sax; I once heard "When the Saints Go Marching In" played at such a slow tempo that for several moments I failed to recognize the tune. Even if the music lent itself to such activity, twisting is forbidden.

Attendance at the dance is understandably minimal, although there are always three or four Chinese couples, who clearly attend under instructions in order to demonstrate the right of Chinese to be on the formerly exclusive premises. For the first two hours they sit in an alcove on one side of the dance floor, each indulging himself to the extent of one orange drink and a few extremely decorous dances. At ten o'clock sharp they rise in a group and solemnly march to the alcove on the other side, where they each enjoy a second orange drink and a few more arms'-length perambulations. As for the few foreigners who attend the dance, they seem equally intimidated by the atmosphere. At any rate, it is the only place where I have ever seen inhibited Cubans.

Foreigners are left largely to their own devices, and entertain each other with dinners and dances in their own homes and embassies. While usually decorous, these sometimes take on an air of desperate gaiety, especially among the younger people. After one fairly wild party at the Druzbha, I walked to my car with one of the foreign teachers. "We are quite lively here," he said. "Some of us are much more lively than we are at home. It's for *their* benefit."

Much of my time in Peking was spent sitting in the bar of the Hsin Chiao Hotel. I lived in the Hsin Chiao, had my office there, and I found the bar a good place for meeting the foreign delegations, businessmen, and tourists who are coming to Peking in growing numbers and who mostly stay in the same hotel. And while this tiny bar has little to offer in the way of charm and atmosphere, consisting as it does of five small tables wedged in among the elevators, the dining room, and the billiard tables at the top of the hotel, it is one of the two places in China (the other is the airport bar) where you can buy a local concoction which bears the name Martini.

It should be explained that with the occasional exception of Russian vodka, foreign drinks are not on sale in China—which explains why much of the diplomatic baggage from Hong Kong is largely liquid—thus posing a problem for any serious drinker. Of the traditional Chinese beverages, Hsiao Hsin, the hot yellow rice wine served in tiny saucers, cleverly complements a Chinese banquet but is out of place on any other occasion. As for the colorless liquid known as Mao Tai, this is an outrageous device of incredible strength, apparently devised by the Chinese for the sole purpose of drinking their foreign guests under the table—an undertaking they gleefully carry out through the medium of endless friendly toasts,

each concluded with the ringing salutation *"Gampei!"*
("Bottoms up")—while on their part they often cheat by
merely sipping.

Of late the Chinese have begun to emulate Western
beverages, partly for the benefit of their export trade.
Their table wines hardly merit serious discussion, and
while their vodka and brandy are possibly palatable, their
whisky smells like paint remover and is a total disaster.
Chinese beer, however, is generally excellent, especially
the brand from the old German brewery at Tsingtao and
one of the Peking brews. It is not so good in the south,
where the Canton beer lacks body and the Yunnan beer
tastes of celery.

To my eternal gratitude, the Hsin Chiao bar boasts a
curious mixture of Chinese gin and Chinese vermouth.
Called "Ma-ti-ni" (the literal translation of the Chinese
characters is "Horse-holding-a-nun") and kept ready-
mixed and refrigerated in old whisky bottles, it bears only
scant resemblance to its Western namesake, having a
unique taste and being the color of a strong whisky and
water. But Horse-holding-a-nun is fairly smooth on the
palate and has an encouraging potency. What it did to my
liver I shudder to think, but it kept me going through
many a dreary day.

There was always action in the Hsin Chiao. On a
typical evening I was sitting in the bar, drinking the
inevitable Martini with three visiting journalists—Swiss,
Dutch, and Norwegian. Nearby an Albanian footballer
was talking to an Italian television producer, and other
Albanians were playing billiards with guttural shouts of
glee and chagrin. Suddenly the elevators opened to disgorge the female members of a dance troupe from Guinea,
on their way to the dining room for an after-show snack.
Under towering multicolored headdresses they gently un-
dulated past us, their ample dark bodies making a surge of
vitality and sensuality amid the drab surroundings. At the

next table a party of Dutch businessmen, negotiating the sale of a chemical fertilizer plant, burst into spontaneous applause. With this the dancers stopped, and gravely shook all our hands. As they swept on again my Norwegian colleague stood rubbing his right hand with his left, a bemused expression on his face.

"That was good," he sighed. "After five weeks in China, that was very good."

Living in the Hsin Chiao, I never knew what to expect in the way of spectacle. On another day four tiny and delicate Nepalese in exquisite embroidered caps sat in the dining room and watched in wonder a parade of giants and giantesses, blond and towering. Each morning these volleyball players from the Soviet Union kept a dozen Chinese waiters and waitresses rushing from the kitchen with endless plates piled high with mountains of eggs, frankfurters, pancakes, toast, and apples. And what did these same waiters and waitresses think of the ballet troupe from Cuba, and especially of the slim young boy and girl, poured into the tightest of trousers, who greeted each other in the middle of the same dining room with the most extravagant and theatrical of gestures, then clung in a passionate embrace that seemed to last for several minutes? The Chinese waiters and waitresses watched in wide-eyed amazement and then whispered furtively among themselves. Try telling them that Cubans are serious in their socialism.

Then there were the track-and-field athletes from Indonesia, especially the nubile maidens who practiced their running—up and down the corridor outside my office— clad in nothing but the flimsiest of underwear, and making it somewhat difficult for me to concentrate on a sober analysis of Chinese economic problems. Speaking of underwear, the hotel was almost always half-filled with Japanese businessmen doggedly pursuing their dream of a vast market of seven hundred million or more Chinese consumers, and in the summer months lying on their beds in nothing but their drawers, with their doors open and their fans blowing hard, giving the hotel the atmosphere and aroma of some multistory Turkish bath.

There is something about the Hsin Chiao and its cosmopolitan clientele that seems to engender curious mishaps. For several days I was on almost constant call and spent many hours rescuing a gray-haired Canadian grandmother—still attractive, but also dignified and highly alarmed—from the clutches of an equally mature Levantine merchant who kept chasing her along the corridors, draping her with jewelry, and making rather plaintive boasts about his residual virility (in the end, virtue triumphed, and, anyway, the jewels were clearly paste).

Amid the babble of many tongues conversation in the Hsin Chiao was often bitter, as the visitors bemoaned their many frustrations. Tourists, it is true, were generally content. On their rapid cycle of the nine open cities—Canton, Peking, Tientsin, Wuhan, Nanking, Shanghai, Hangchow, Soochow, and Wushi (commonly known to residents as the Milk Run)—they were usually kept too busy to have much time for grousing. With businessmen it was a different story, and time hung heavily on their hands. For some reason—an Oriental indifference to time, monumental inefficiency, or perhaps a desire to teach the foreigner his place—few businessmen are able to complete their transactions with any sort of dispatch. Meetings with the Chinese state trading corporations are often days apart; in between the trader dares not leave his hotel room for fear the phone will ring. As one European businessman put it, "Now I know how callgirls feel."

Chinese officials would be pained to hear such complaints. They would maintain, with some justification, that much is done to assure the ease and comfort of every visitor, especially in terms of interpreters, transport, adequate hotels, lavish banquets, and guided tours of communes, factories, and other institutions. Behind the scenes even greater efforts are devoted to insuring that the visitor receives a favorable impression and is not embarrassed or discomfited in any way. Before National Day a document by no less a personage than Foreign Minister Chen Yi is distributed and read among the population of Peking. It tells the citizens that many foreign guests will be arriving for the ceremonies and that their strange habits, including their propensity for taking pictures in the streets, must be tolerated. A similar document was circulated around the schools and universities just before the arrival of a delegation of nearly three hundred young Japanese, mostly from Communist and other left-wing organizations. While massive posters around the capital proclaimed the unbreakable solidarity between Chinese and Japanese youth, this document admitted that there might, in fact, be certain differences. It pointed out that the Japanese would be wearing pointed shoes, tight trousers, and other bourgeois clothing, but must not be stared at or ridiculed on this account. Nor were they to be engaged in conversation, except by their official guides. However, nothing was left to chance, and it was conceded that the Japanese themselves might open conversation. To cover this eventuality, the document listed all the likely questions they might ask—including "Why is China conducting nuclear tests?" and "Why is China feuding with the Soviet Union?"—and then outlined in detail the answers that were to be given.

Such thoroughness is a mark of Chinese dealings with the foreigner. Some days after he moved into a new apartment at San Li Tun, a young diplomat noticed that his rooms were rapidly filling up with cockroaches. At first the Chinese denied even the possibility of such a mishap, but later, forced to face the fact of walls that were crawling with the beasts, they agreed to have the apartment fumigated. In the meantime a meeting was clearly held to discuss the embarrassing event and to determine the proper response. Within the space of two days the diplomat received the same explanation on separate occasions from half a dozen Chinese—his office interpreter, his amah, his language teacher, his driver, the building superintendent, and the pest removers—each of whom told him in almost identical words that the cockroaches must have come from Hong Kong in the packing of his cases; at any rate, they could not possibly be Chinese.

Of all the foreigners in China it is probably the Africans who suffer most. Unlike many Europeans, few have any experience of surviving amid such difficult circumstances, and most feel badly hampered by the drabness of their life and the lack of entertainment. For many weeks I played billiards in the bar of the Hsin Chiao with an African who was spending several months in China on a cultural scholarship. A husky man in the prime of his life, he was suffering badly from the lack of female companionship. Well aware that nothing of that sort could be had in China, he suggested a cultural tour that would take him as far south as Canton. When his Chinese hosts readily agreed, he added that while in Canton, he would like to cross over to Hong Kong for a few days. Impossible, said the horrified Chinese. But why, asked my friend, pointing out that a visa would be no problem. Ah, yes, said the Chinese, but, you see, we couldn't guarantee your safety in Hong Kong.

Then there were the soldiers from another African country who arrived in Peking after many months of training at the Chinese guerrilla school at Wuhan. On a chance visit to their embassy a colleague of mine met these tall, husky, unsmiling, and extremely formidable warriors. Making idle conversation, he asked them what they would do on reaching home. One of them growled, "Get the man who sent us here!"

North of Peking the Great Wall undulates across the hills like some monstrous snake or dragon. Broad enough on top so that six horsemen could ride abreast, it crosses four provinces and stretches for seventeen hundred miles on its way to the sea. Each time I climbed it I was awed by a fresh appreciation of the mentality of its creators, for the Wall, too, is part of the Middle Kingdom outlook. The Chinese were willing to receive tribute-bearing envoys from some barbarian lands. But against the rude tribesmen to the north they built this massive structure of brick and granite, convinced that it would forever protect their civilization from contamination.

Today the Chinese look outward. Instead of walling out some barbarians and waiting for others to come bearing tribute, they seek actively to impose their revolutionary pattern on the world. Their uncompromising fervor can be explained in part by the demands of a messianic Communism which is always strongest in those, like the present Chinese rulers, who have made their own revolution. But much, I suspect, is also explained by the same innate feelings of racial and cultural superiority. China, to its rulers, is still the Middle Kingdom, and in time all the peoples of the world will come to acknowledge the excellence of its ways and agree to follow China's lead.

When the Chinese leaders lavish their impressive hospitality on Afro–Asian leaders, they make ringing speeches about friendship, equality, sovereignty, and non-interference. But Chinese actions in the Afro–Asian world have often exposed the hypocrisy of these sentiments, and it is hard to escape the feeling that even today the Chinese regard these visitors as vassals bearing tribute. The old pattern reasserts itself when someone like Prince Sihanouk of Cambodia makes his annual pilgrimage to Peking, praises Chinese achievements, and pledges his allegiance. In return, the Chinese seem to employ the three cardinal virtues of leadership, as expressed by a classic Han Dynasty saying: "To simulate affection, to express honeyed sentiments, and to treat one's inferiors as equals."

Traditional patterns also come to the fore when the Chinese wish to reject overtures from nations or individuals with whom they have some quarrel. Here the old arrogance reasserts itself in the rude violence of their language. When China refused a visa to Patrick Gordon-Walker, the former British Foreign Secretary who was undertaking a peace mission over Vietnam, the *People's Daily* boasted that China had "slammed the door" in his face. The United Nations Secretary-General, U Thant, was also told that he would not be welcome in Peking, and that "obviously, he is knocking at the wrong door." Discussing the election to the Security Council of the so-called neo-colonialist state of Malaysia, the Chinese said, "This is like shitting on one's head, while holding a sword at one's throat." At different times Nikita Khrushchev has been called a "clown," Harold Wilson a "nitwit" and his government a "voluntary political pimp" of the United States, Lyndon Johnson a "driveler," and the new Soviet leaders "monsters" and a "handful of wretches."

Experts in the Chinese tongue often excuse these excesses by pointing out that it is a Chinese literary custom to heighten language in order to convey a certain mood, and that such violent epithets should not be taken literally. On the other hand, a visiting correspondent questioned a *People's Daily* editor on this point and received an earnest assurance that such insults were not selected in any haphazard manner. On the contrary, there was always much discussion, and a careful grading of epithets—"for instance, we would never call the British Prime Minister a gangster; that description we reserve for the President of the United States."

I suspect that such rough language is best explained by the same feelings of superiority. It is only natural to speak crudely to barbarians, as was made clear by a placard that appeared in Canton in 1844, denouncing the British:

> Our hatred is already at white heat. If we do not completely exterminate you pigs and dogs, we will not be manly Chinese able to support the sky on our heads and stand firmly on the earth. . . .
>
> We are definitely going to kill you, cut your heads off, and burn you to death! . . . We must strip off your skins and eat your flesh, and then you will know how tough we are. . . .
>
> *We ought really to use refined expressions. But since you beasts do not understand written characters, therefore we use rough, vulgar words to instruct you in simple terms. . . .* (Emphasis added)

As recently as early 1965 China seemed to be moving from one success to another in its double drive to win leadership of both the Communist and Afro–Asian worlds. Within the ranks of international Communism the Soviet Union was still staggering from the abrupt dismissal of Nikita Khrushchev (which confirmed a long-standing Chinese prophecy), and the flood of pro-Peking parties and splinter groups was on the rise. Bolstered by their first atomic explosions and the earlier triumphant safaris of Premier Chou En-lai, the Chinese seemed on the brink of uniting the Afro–Asian nations into a militant bloc which would follow the leadership of Peking in opposition to both the United States and the Soviet Union.

Then the roof fell in, and the rest of 1965 saw a steady series of reverses for Peking, with the fall of Ben Bella in

Algiers, the fiasco of the second Afro–Asian Conference, the debacle of Chou's later tours and the growing aversion of African leaders to his call for revolution, the mishandled Chinese intervention in the Indo–Pakistani war, the bungled pro-Communist coup in Indonesia, and the rift with Cuba. In Communist affairs in general, the Chinese were thrust on the defensive, as the Soviet Union, with its leaders showing more subtlety than Khrushchev, recovered lost ground and even lost allies.

There were many reasons for these setbacks, including the American determination to fight on in Vietnam (which at least demonstrated that the U.S. was not quite the paper tiger that Peking claimed it was), and the more skillful tactics of Moscow. To some extent, too, they must be explained by the heavy-handed approach of the Chinese to the Afro–Asian world, as exemplified by Chou En-lai's oft-repeated assertion that Africa was "ripe for revolution"—a statement which alarmed even so veteran a revolutionary as Kenya's Jomo Kenyatta. The Chinese seem to suffer partly from their lack of experience in the outside world—with the exception of Chou En-lai and Chen Yi, few of the top leaders have ever been farther afield than Moscow—and partly from a case of bad reporting on the part of Chinese diplomats and other agents overseas. Chinese abroad lead isolated lives and rarely venture beyond their compounds. It is also tempting to suspect that the Chinese diplomats' reports from foreign nations emulate the example of Chinese viceroys and other local officials under earlier dynasties. Describing conditions inside China, these latter would almost always tell the Dragon Throne what it wanted to hear, rather than what was really happening, for fear of invoking Imperial wrath.

But to a large extent China's failures seem linked to the traditional Chinese view of the outside world. Never in their history have the Chinese worked within a framework of allies and alliances. Traditionally they have known only one basic diplomatic link: that of a single vassal state which pledged allegiance to Peking. They are accustomed to dealing with individual nations one at a time; even today, Chinese officials in Peking will only go to diplomatic parties, other than National Day celebrations, on the tacit understanding that foreigners from no other country will be present, and a diplomat who breaks this rule will find that his Chinese guests sulk, and seldom accept another invitation. Unused to the give-and-take of alliance diplomacy, the Chinese seem happiest when a statesman like Prince Sihanouk conforms to the traditional pattern. When their messianic Communism drives them toward domination of Afro–Asian and Communist councils, they prove incapable of compromising their militant doctrines, unable to accept a partnership of equals, and determined to turn the whole alliance into a single vassal which accepts the leadership of Peking.

This is certainly true of relations with the Soviet Union. During their twenty-eight-year struggle for power the Chinese Communists received little material assistance from the Russians. Even more crucial, they frequently found their interests sacrificed by Stalin in order to further the goals of Soviet foreign policy. The newly victorious Chinese Communists linked their destiny with the Soviet Union in the 1949–50 period because they had little choice, in view of their economic needs and the hostility and suspicion of most Western powers, especially the United States.

Significantly, it was the first time in history that any Chinese regime had opted for such an alliance. Subsequent events gave the Chinese little reason to feel that the experiment was justified. From the start the Russians drove a hard bargain with their economic and military aid. When the Chinese felt forced to intervene in the Soviet-sponsored Korean War (as United Nations forces,

driving toward the Yalu, threatened China's national interests), the Russians provided only arms and equipment,
for which they extracted heavy payments. Later the
Soviet Union gave China only indifferent support during
the Offshore Islands crisis of 1958, and in his Camp David
meeting with President Eisenhower, Nikita Khrushchev
performed what the Chinese could only regard as an act
which grossly betrayed the Sino–Soviet alliance. Finally,
the Russians abruptly cut off their economic aid and
withdrew their experts in 1960, delivering an extremely
hard blow to the Chinese economy.

If the Chinese are to be believed—and there is evidence
to support their case—Moscow has also stirred up trouble
along the disputed Sino–Soviet border, especially in Sinkiang. There are also some grounds for suspecting that
Khrushchev was conniving against the Chinese leadership
through the medium of Marshal Peng Teh-huai, the Defense Minister who was suddenly sacked in 1959.

Nothing in this sorry record would give the Chinese
much reason to place any trust in alliances. And because
of their Middle Kingdom outlook, the Chinese Communists must have felt uncomfortable from the start about
aligning themselves in a subordinate role with what was
basically a European, or barbarian, movement. As early as
the late 1920's Mao Tse-tung was cheerfully disregarding
orthodox Marxist–Leninist doctrines and Moscow's directives by insisting that the Chinese Revolution must be
based on the peasantry rather than the urban proletariat.
In the 1949–51 period other Chinese leaders claimed
that Mao had added to "the treasury of Marxist–Leninist
thought" and that the Chinese revolution, rather than the
Russian, was the proper model for the Asian, African, and
Latin American world.

With the death of Stalin and the full flowering of
the dispute with Moscow, Mao was openly hailed by
Peking propagandists as the greatest living Marxist–Len-

inist, and the status of the Soviet leaders was scornfully denigrated. With their present bitter polemics the Chinese are not only asserting their double claim to the leadership of both the Communist and the developing worlds; they are also reverting to the traditional position that China is the center of the world, the home of true doctrine, and the model which lesser breeds must emulate. To a striking extent their diatribes against the Russians manifest the same arrogance and self-confidence as did Ch'ien Lung's epistle to George III or any other such Imperial edict. In this position the Chinese are clearly much happier than they were in the years when Stalin was alive and they felt compelled to pay lip service to Soviet leadership.

Today the whole psychology of the Middle Kingdom outlook lies behind each militant Chinese thrust in both the Communist and Afro–Asian worlds. On the one hand the Chinese leaders are dedicated *Communists* who made their revolution with little outside help and who seem to believe sincerely that Mao has reworked Marx and Lenin to provide an inevitable revolutionary pattern for the world. On the other hand they are also *Chinese* with understandable nationalistic ambitions, traditional notions of cultural and racial superiority, and a determination to revive the glories of the Middle Kingdom, when all the known world acknowledged China's sway. In their polemics with the Soviet Union the Chinese continue to condemn "great nation chauvinism" and to profess the deepest feelings for "equality and mutual interest." But as they recoil from China's heavy-handed diplomatic blundering more and more Afro–Asian leaders see the double danger of a militant Communism linked with traditional racial arrogance.

Yet it is foolish to revive fears of the Yellow Peril and to speak, as some Western leaders have, about China's plans for global conquest. Such sentiments are merely the reverse

image of Chinese diatribes against "United States imperialism." Instead, it is important for the West to distinguish between the nationalistic and the ideological components of present Peking drives, and to study what the
Communists have actually done, as opposed to what they
have threatened. For instance, when the Chinese proclaim
the cause of world revolution, and state that the "countryside" of the world (Asia, Africa, and Latin America) will
surround and overwhelm the "cities" (Western Europe
and North America), this is not a blueprint for Chinese
aggression or expansion, although it does encompass Chinese support for native revolutionary movements. Rather,
it is a statement of orthodox Maoism in the Confucian
tradition of proclaiming the True Doctrine, whether or
not it is practically feasible, in order to influence others.
On the other hand, when the Chinese state their determination eventually to "liberate" Taiwan, this is an expression of one of their most fundamental nationalistic
goals, and an issue on which they will brook no compromise.

It is also vital to distinguish between Chinese *statements* (which are undoubtedly fiery) and Chinese *actions*
(which are generally cautious). Since 1949 the Chinese
have not been notably aggressive or expansionist. When
they have used force (as in Korea, Tibet, the Taiwan
Straits, and the Himalayas), it has always been within
clear limitations and only when they felt that their national security or territorial integrity were vitally involved. The Chinese are well aware of their own self-
interest, as in their continued tolerance of colonial and
capitalist Hong Kong, where they earn so much of their
foreign exchange, and in their friendly relations with non-
Communist Pakistan, Cambodia, and Burma. They are
also well aware of their limitations, both military and
economic. They may have blundered badly in the wider
diplomatic scene, but at least around their own borders

the Chinese are realistic and restrained in the exercise of power.

If it is important to get away from outdated Cold War concepts, it is also vital to abandon any unrealistic, sentimental attachment to the China-that-was. American leaders especially seem to judge China too often in terms of a Communist conspiracy that has usurped power over a lovable people who remain fundamentally anti-Communist in terms of their traditional background of Confucian piety, family loyalties, and conservative and individualistic traits. In a very real sense official American outlooks are a reverse image of the Chinese contention that "We love the great American people; it is only the narrow American ruling class that we hate and oppose." If this sounds strange to Americans, so must the Chinese wonder at Lyndon Johnson's reference, in a 1964 speech, to "our historic friends, the talented and courageous Chinese people on the mainland."

This position is both unrealistic and dangerous, since it ignores or underestimates the nationalistic impulses that are shared by many Chinese who have no love of Communism and that will still be virulent long after Chinese Communism has become milder and even "revisionist."

4

Puritans
and Ping-Pong

Cheerful children at play.

While the parents work, an old man wheels his grandson in a crude carriage in a Peking park.

In Peking's Tien An Men Square an officious cadre prevents a visiting cameraman from filming the elaborate logistics of a "spontaneous demonstration."

Despite a chill autumn drizzle, bare-limbed girl swimmers step out smartly in a Peking parade marking the anniversary of China's Communist government.

Young girls dance in tumultuous welcome of an African head-of-state.

Once this girl might have been a slave or a concubine. Today, a proud member of the militia, she totes an automatic rifle.

At a part work-part study school outside Canton, young peasants learn the anatomy of a cow.

Opposite. Workers in a Sian factory attend a political meeting after coming off shift. Such meetings are a regular feature of life for most Chinese.

Peasants on a crowded commune street near Shanghai.

Opposite. "Down With U.S. Imperialism!" In a demonstration outside the North Vietnamese Embassy in Peking, Chinese actors dressed as Vietnamese guerrillas overcome other Chinese actors portraying cowering American soldiers.

Far from the tourist's beaten track, old men relax in a Peking hutung.

Chinese communes slowly enter the modern era. Near Taiyuan, peasants use an electrically-run corn husker.

Food supplies in the cities are now ample, if hardly lavish. On the main shopping street Pekinese sample a juicy watermelon crop.

As the British-built Viscount banked down through the clouds, the stewardess told us to fasten our seatbelts and then began a lengthy tirade: "We are now approaching Shanghai. This is where the imperialists began to oppress the Chinese people. . . ."

Later my earnest young interpreter showed me the park which allegedly had the infamous sign, No Dogs or Chinese (old-timers insist that the actual wording was never quite so blatant), and assured me that before the Communist victory no Chinese woman could walk along the Bund at night for fear of being raped by drunken American sailors. Then he took me to the Great World, the five-story amusement center in the old French Concession, where foreigners went for girls, boys, cards, and opium. In his own graphic words, "With its gamblers, prostitutes, pockpickets [sic], local despots, and other dirty things, the Great World was a miniature of old Shanghai." Today, of course, all that is changed, and I watched thousands of Chinese enjoying jugglers, acrobats, and patriotic operas with apparent pleasure and total decorum.

My nights in Shanghai were, understandably, hardly eventful, for as part of the new moral order the Chinese shield their women from grasping foreign hands. Proud of their independence yet traumatized by their past humilia-

tion by European powers, they are determined that foreigners in new China should behave themselves. These
feelings are expressed most forcefully in Shanghai, where
the foreigners had their largest concessions and greatest
privileges.

Nowhere is the change more obvious than at the spa-
cious four-story house on the Bund that is the home of
The Longest Bar in the World. Once the ultra-exclusive
Shanghai Club, favorite rendezvous of bankers, diplomats,
and other members of the Occidental elite, today the
famous bar (it measures about 100 feet) is still intact, but
the "imperialists" have been expelled, and the building is
now a Social Club for Chinese and Foreign Seamen.

"We shut the bar at eleven P.M.," said Mr. Ling, Vice-
Director of the Club, young, bespectacled, and very intent. "This is so the sailors can get back to their ships,
have a good rest, and work well the next day."

It was evident that any ambiguity in Mr. Ling's official
title was strictly in my mind. Here, as elsewhere in the
sprawling port, the entertainment is rigorously healthy. In
the basement Mr. Ling showed me ping-pong tables and a
shooting gallery. On the ground floor there was a reading
room stocked with Chinese magazines and political pamphlets in many languages, including such current favor-
ites as "On Khrushchev's Phony Communism and its Historical Lessons for the World." Hardly anyone was using
the library, but there was a good crowd of European
sailors watching a movie in the theater upstairs. As we
looked in, a young Chinese girl and boy were staring
misty-eyed from the screen—it was the climax of a love
scene, and they were at least five feet apart. Nearby a
notice advertised the next attraction: "Premier Chou En-
lai in Albania—a Colorful Documentary Film."

Nor was this the limit to the entertainment provided by
the Club. With growing enthusiasm, Mr. Ling explained
that visits were arranged to factories, workers' living

quarters, and industrial exhibits. "Above all," he added, "we know that after so many weeks at sea the sailors want to see grass and flowers. So we arrange visits to parks and gardens."

Surely, I suggested, some of the foreign sailors might show livelier inclinations?

Yes, Mr. Ling agreed, sometimes they drink too much: "Then we try gentle persuasion. We ask them to take less drink because we're concerned for their health. Sometimes they don't understand this, and go on drinking. Sometimes they even hit our staff members. But we just go on persuading. Sometimes they are sick. Then we help them to bed. While they're asleep, we wash their clothes. When they wake up the next morning, we tell them what happened and show them their clean clothes, and then they are greatly moved."

I remarked that in other ports I had visited sailors had occasionally been known to seek out female companionship.

Mr. Ling laughed. "This is a very common question which we often get from the seamen of capitalist countries."

What was the answer?

"First, we tell them that this is a socialist country, so there can be nothing like that. Then we do our best to meet their just requests—to see football matches, acrobatic performances, and so on. We lead them toward a healthy spare-time life."

Warming to his subject, Mr. Ling told about a West German sailor who had made such an improper request: "We explained the situation, and then we led him to the ping-pong room. Every night he came back to play ping-pong, and when he left, he told us he had never enjoyed himself so much in any port, and never spent so little money."

I asked if Communist sailors ever raised the same

subject. Mr. Ling's answer neatly fitted the Chinese charge of creeping revisionism in the Soviet Union and its allies: "Not in the past," he said. "Lately some individuals from socialist countries have started to ask this question. Of course, they don't ask it straight out like the seamen from capitalist countries, but we know their meaning."

Did they get treated in the same way?

"They get the same explanation," said Mr. Ling, "and," he added sternly, "they also get criticism."

Sometimes, it appears, not all the foreign sailors are pacified by ping-pong or cowed by criticism. Shortly after the Chinese opened their new port at Hsinkang, outside Tientsin, they were visited by an Eastern European freighter. Scrambling aboard, Chinese officials asked politely how they could entertain the crew. To a man the sailors requested a dance. Somewhat taken back, the Chinese consulted among themselves, and then allowed it could be done, but would take twenty-four hours to arrange.

Next evening several dozen husky seamen put on their best clothes and went ashore. In the seamen's club they found a bar well stocked with Chinese beverages, an orchestra tuning up, and the same polite Chinese officials, all dressed alike in their blue and gray high-collared tunics. But the girls had not arrived. For an hour the sailors drank steadily at the bar and engaged in desultory conversation with their hosts. Nine o'clock, and still no girls.

"When does the dance begin?" they asked.

"In a minute," beamed the Chinese.

Suddenly the band struck up a martial strain, and each sailor was solemnly approached by a Chinese man. "Will you dance?" they asked.

The sailors wrecked the place, of course. A few days

later an official from their embassy in Peking was summoned to the Foreign Ministry and sternly presented with a bill for the damages.

As a fairly firm rule, no foreigner is allowed to dally with a Chinese girl, but there are occasional exceptions: a few diplomats from friendly countries and a few foreigners working for the Chinese government have been permitted Chinese brides, but often only after they had persevered against officialdom for several months.

There is a frequent rumor, inside and outside China, that Chinese girls are officially provided for favored Asian and African visitors, and that there are even brothels for this purpose. I can only report that I found no evidence to support this rumor, and that given Chinese obsessions on this point, I doubt whether it has much basis in fact. I do know of several cases in which, acting on their own, foreigners in China have managed to acquire a Chinese girl friend. They are almost invariably discovered, and almost always the outcome is tragic, with the girl shipped off to the countryside for an indefinite period. The fate of the man seems to depend on China's relations with his country. I know of one or two from friendly countries who escaped with only a warning. Then there was the engineer from a "revisionist" Eastern European nation whom I met one night in the bar of the Hsin Chiao. As we sipped our brandies he told me that after several months of work on a construction project, he was on his way back home.

"Are you glad to be going?" I asked.

"Of course," he said. "But it is also sad."

"Why?"

"You see, I am leaving two friends behind."

"For how long?"

"For seven years. You see, they were caught with Chinese girls."

It is not only the foreigner who suffers from this new puritanism, for the stern regulation of sexual activity has become a major part of the Chinese Communist ethic. This has involved considerable rethinking by the Chinese leaders, as well as some rewriting of the official record.

In the early years of the revolution, Mao Tse-tung and his colleagues had a distinct romantic streak, for all their adherence to a doctrine of hard work and plain living. At first their attitudes were liberal, almost bohemian. Attacking the system of arranged marriages in an article written in 1919, Mao salutes "the tidal wave of the freedom to love." Describing the habits of peasants in his native province in his famous Hunan Report of 1927, he writes, "They also enjoy considerable sexual freedom. Among the poor peasantry, triangular and multilateral relationships are almost universal."

But today these passages have been removed from Mao's *Collected Works*. Far from advocating sexual freedom, the Chinese leaders now decree the repression and sublimation of all such urges. Seeking to impose their discipline on the Chinese masses, determined to eradicate all "bourgeois" and "revisionist" tendencies, these romantic revolutionaries have become the sternest of puritans.

From the moment they enter China foreigners are made aware of this new dispensation. They see it, first of all, in the women. These shapeless bundles seem members of some Orwellian Anti-Sex League. With their baggy shirts and slacks, each seems determined to disguise and even to disown her feminine charms. How else to explain the mutilations practiced on their lovely, glossy, jet-black tresses—now either scissored short in the plainest of trims, or else constricted in pigtails hanging down from floppy caps.

Sometimes you see exceptions, depending partly on the seasons. In the North in the winter men and women alike bundle themselves into blue cotton-padded uniforms, sexless but practical. With the warmer weather there is more diversity in dress, and on a summer day in Peking you can see signs that the Chinese have not lost all feeling for fashion—perhaps a young girl walking down the Wang Fu Ching, the main shopping street, with a red ribbon in her hair, a pretty patterned blouse, and slacks that are slightly tapered. In the past she might have been in trouble for adorning herself in even such a tentative way. When I first arrived in China, officials in Shanghai were whipping up a big campaign against a lady who had an argument with her tailor. She asked him to make her slacks tighter around the hips and more tapered in the legs. He stoutly refused to make such "bizarre" clothing, and his praises were sung in the newspapers and at hundreds of meetings called in factories and offices to discuss this vital question.

Later, however, the line began to change. No less an authority than the editor of the *People's Daily* ruled that since standards of living were improving and more people had more money, it was permitted to wear brighter, fancier clothes. Even permanent waves, he added, were not necessarily signs of a bourgeois outlook.

Yet few seem willing to take him at his word. The women still dress like men and walk like men, and often you can be sure of the sex only by the pigtail. This spectacle so distressed a distinguished Asian visitor that he shocked his hosts by blurting in anguish, "What have you done with the women's breasts—cut them off?" Yet that was hardly fair, for the Chinese girl is not noted for her mamillary development. Many foreigners have a conception of the Chinese female that is based upon the fragile beauties on ancient scrolls, the elaborately adorned heroines of Peking Opera, or the silk-sheathed bargirls of Hong Kong and Singapore—a conception as unrealistic as it is romantic.

The Chinese point out that it is traditional for most Chinese women to wear trousers, especially in the countryside. They add that the clinging cheongsam is of alien, Manchu origin, and was only introduced in recent times. And in a country where most women work, tackling almost every job, loose-fitting, hard-wearing, comfortable clothes are a practical necessity.

By downgrading woman's sexual role, the Chinese also seek to emphasize her new social and political emancipation. Gone are the days of foot-binding and arranged marriages, of daughters sold as slaves and prostitutes. Chinese women, it is stated, have new rights, new responsibilities, and new dignity, and are no longer the playthings of the domineering male. Now, they are completely equal (well—almost—since there is still only a small proportion of women in higher government and Party ranks. Here, perhaps, the Chinese leaders are unconsciously fighting a last-ditch battle for male supremacy).

This emancipated attitude was firmly stated by a lady interpreter in Sian, the capital of Shensi province. She was charming, but also very strong-minded and determined in her outlook. In the course of our trips around the city I learned that she was a Party member, married to a teacher of Russian who was also a Party member, and that they had three children. When I was about to fly on to Yenan, the old revolutionary base, she said she would go with me because there were no interpreters there. Since it would be a two- or three-day trip, I apologized for taking her away from her family.

Not at all, she answered briskly. Her duty to me came first. Besides, her mother-in-law would take care of the children, and as for the cooking and the housework, her husband always did that anyway. It seemed that while everyone in the family wore trousers, there was no doubt about who was really in charge.

Then there was the leader of an all-girl militia squad at

a textile factory on the outskirts of Canton. For my benefit she marched her troupe around the courtyard, shouting orders in a clear, crisp voice. Later, as she sipped tea with me, her rifle between her knees, I asked her if she had any trouble with such a military, non-feminine role.

Her reply was prompt and scornful. "In new China, men and women are completely equal. We despise those pompous ladies who know only how to decorate themselves."

Even movie stars have the same outlook. In Changchun, at China's second largest film studio, I met the closest Chinese equivalent to a Hollywood starlet. Her name was Ching Di, and she had a very pretty smile. But in her floppy jacket and trousers she looked like any Chinese girl. And far from enjoying the sybaritic whirl of a Western movie star, she had just returned from a six-month stint in a peasant village.

"I'm taking the lead in a movie about how democratic reforms came to a minority village in Yunnan," she said. "But I'm a city girl, and I don't know much about peasants. So I went to live with them and work with them, to understand their outlook."

Already well known across China, Ching Di often goes out with troupes of other actors to give performances in factories and communes. I described how a Western star, such as Elizabeth Taylor, would be mobbed by her fans on such occasions. Ching Di listened with an expression of mild disdain on her pretty face.

"Oh, nothing like that ever happens to us. Of course, the people often recognize us and sometimes get excited."

And what wild forms does their excitement take?

"Well, they come up and shake our hands, and ask us how we are, and what movie we're making now. You see," Ching Di added earnestly, "their interest is very natural, because we're so close to the masses."

At Changchun they also showed me a new movie, in the

style of local opera, which demonstrated the new priorities for women, at the same time seeming to reveal the
unconscious tensions that result from sexual repression.
Its subject was a young peasant girl, jealous of her brother
since he was in the militia and had a rifle. Seizing his
rifle, she first caressed it and then hugging it to her
breast, did a dance. When her brother snatched it away,
she did another dance with an equally symbolic broom
handle, aiming it at apples on a tree, and singing that she
was shooting at the head of Chiang Kai-shek.

Any psychoanalyst would have been intrigued, but the
Chinese movie makers, concerned only with the political
moral, seemed unaware of any deeper implications. This
was given by grandad, who came over the hill with a
shiny new automatic rifle. Rejecting his offer of a pretty
red dress and demanding the rifle instead, the girl seized
it and did another loving dance.

Eventually the old man gave in and handed over the
weapon. His closing line: "Remember, there are two-
thirds of the people of the world who are still not liber-
ated. You must follow the Chinese Communist Party and
hold the rifle high."

In a new China bursting to be built there simply isn't
time for sex—or so officials would like us to believe. This
opinion was echoed in a Peking University dormitory,
where I interviewed six boys and girls, all in their early
twenties and their fourth year of a five-year English
course. When I asked them what they did for relaxation,
they mentioned swimming, boating, and a movie once a
week.

In the West, I said, undergraduates spent a lot of time
dating. Did they know what that meant?

Yes, they knew about dating. In fact, said the quietest
and most serious boy, they could date each other if they
wanted to.

"Would dating couples be ridiculed or punished?"

"No," he answered firmly.

But the others took a different line. Said a second boy, "We don't date because we have to save our energies. First, we must have knowledge so we can serve the people better when we graduate."

Said a stern-faced young girl with large glasses, "We live here together like brother and sister."

That was too much for the young administrative director of the university, who saw that I was getting an impression that was not entirely favorable.

"All the same," he told the prettiest girl, "I bet you have a secret love."

"Oh!" she exclaimed, widening her beautiful black eyes and shaking her silken pigtails. She looked horrified, then giggled, but said nothing more. It might be true, but she wasn't letting on.

Officials also regard dating with suspicion since it can lead young comrades off the proper proletarian path. With evident dismay a Canton newspaper complained that some young workers "dress or pretty up for dating and romancing until late at night." The newspaper warned sternly that they might become corrupt and degenerate, and fall prey to class enemies spreading bourgeois and capitalist ideas. It suggested that young people should study the *Works* of Chairman Mao, build up their bodies through physical exercise, watch plays and movies, and visit parks. In the same vein, the magazine *Chinese Women* said, "Young people now need the revolutionary emotions of the proletariat, not the vulgar soft perceptions of the bourgeoisie." It defined these latter as "walking with the loved one arm in arm, in parks and on streets, in cinemas, at dances, in restaurants; also, caressing, fondling, gazing at each other, and prattling about love."

As dating is discouraged, so are early marriages, and partly for the same reason—so that young people can devote themselves fully to their studies (another reason,

less publicized, is the need to keep the population down).
On communes and in cities across China, in dozens of
conversations with young men and women, I received the
same standard reply: "We don't think of getting married
yet. We must finish our studies, go where the Party sends
us, and work hard for the people."

By law men can marry at twenty and girls at eighteen.
In practice men are usually "persuaded" to hold off until
they are twenty-nine or thirty and girls until they are
twenty-five or twenty-six, although special dispensations
are sometimes given to army officers and Party cadres.
Youngsters insisting on their legal rights usually find such
"persuasion" overwhelming. At their homes, at their
schools or places of work, Party officials and even their
closest friends join in putting on the pressure, and it is
usually effective. Sometimes it is overcome, but young
people who insist on marrying short of the approved age
can find themselves speedily shipped to different parts of
the country.

When it comes to choosing a partner, comrades are told
to abjure bourgeois concepts of romantic love and seek
out someone with a correct political viewpoint. An issue
of *Chinese Women* carried a letter from Chen Mei-ying, a
young girl in a workshop of the Foochow shipbuilding
yards. As Mei-ying told the tale, she fell in love with Chen
Huan, the twenty-eight-year-old chairman of the factory
trade union, and obviously a Party stalwart. But he was
crippled, and their fellow workers gossiped: "It is really
like throwing a beautiful flower on a pile of cow dung"—
or so Mei-ying wrote, with no apparent modesty. Her
parents also tried to veto the match, hoping to arrange a
marriage to someone with a bigger income. They appealed to the authorities, claiming that poor Huan had
seduced their daughter.

But officials took the young couple's side and the head
of the local women's federation sternly told the parents

that looks and wealth were unimportant and that, "to look for a husband for your daughter, the most important thing is to see whether or not that man is progressive in his thinking."

However absurd such stories may sound to a Westerner, it should be remembered that such directives mark an emancipating advance from the old custom whereby parents arranged the marriages of their children, thinking mainly of the wealth involved and little of their offsprings' feelings. It is the same with the marriage ceremony, which was always meant to be lavish and often put families into debt for years. Today these ceremonies must be simple, even spartan. This, at any rate, is the intention, although attacks in the press indicate that old habits die hard, especially in the countryside.

In the cities the ideal ceremony is held under the auspices of the factory or office, rather than those of the couple's families. Quite often the parents do not attend, since they may live in other parts of the country. Instead, a few close friends and workmates will gather for a small tea party in the sitting room or living quarters of the organization. They celebrate with candy and cakes, and usually hear a senior official wish the happy pair a brilliant revolutionary future.

On such occasions lavish gifts are discouraged. With great approval Radio Peking broadcast the story of the wedding of Tan Kan-mei, a member of a women's militia battalion in Honan province. Kan-mei refused to receive any expensive presents; all she wanted were "the *Selected Works of Mao Tse-tung*, a night soil pail, and a wooden rifle."

In their attitude to marriage the Communists are partly concerned with undermining the authority of the family. This campaign is waged with great persistence, as witness the praise heaped upon a nineteen-year-old peasant girl in

Hupeh province, who put the finger on her wicked uncle. *China Youth Daily* told how the girl, Tang Yu-lien, grew suspicious of her uncle, Tang Chiu-chiang—"a man seriously affected by bourgeois thought." Uncle Tang had been elected deputy leader of his production team and worked in the team's brewery. His niece became curious when she saw that he had wine at every meal and always returned from the market with lots of meat. Encouraged by her father, she started spying on her uncle. One day, when the rest of the peasants were out in the fields, she caught him cold—sneaking off to market with two buckets of the team's wine.

Uncle Tang tried persuasion and then threats—"If you dare spoil my reputation, I'll break your jaw and tear your mouth wide open!"—but his niece refused to cover up for him. Grabbing the buckets with one hand and her uncle with the other, she shouted, "You dare to rob the collective. Of course, I dare to mind your business. You have stolen wine and evaded tax. I won't allow you to get away with it!"

According to the newspaper, Uncle Tang was sternly punished and his niece was praised for "her exemplary act of impartiality." The editor urged all young people to "learn from Tang Yu-lien her clear-cut class stand of whom to love and whom to hate."

If anyone was shocked that the girl had ratted on a relative, the newspaper failed to report the fact. But the moral was clear: in new China, loyalty to the collective outweighs loyalty to the family. It seems that women still need some convincing, in spite of their new emancipation. At any rate, the director of the women workers department of the Peking General Trade Union felt obliged to complain in the columns of the *Workers' Daily* that some married women were still too family-conscious. "They devote too much attention to household chores and to children, and often ask for leave and stop working for the sake of children and household affairs."

Above all, she wrote, women must get their priorities straight. "To a revolutionary, compared with revolutionary ideals and revolutionary work, household chores and children are secondary. . . . We should know clearly that our work comes first, and household chores come second."

Actually, the Communist rulers have never tried to wipe out the family unit, as scare stories in the West have often stated. For centuries the Chinese family was the main stabilizing factor in a nation that was often wracked by political and economic turmoil. But it was also often an instrument of injustice and tyranny, with the old dominating the young and the men dominating the women. As such it was under attack and starting to disintegrate several decades before the Communist victory.

As a conservative force in society, the family was a prime target for the Communists; but they have sought to eliminate its reactionary influence, not to eradicate the whole system. Young people are taught to resist their parents and their grandparents when they advocate such bourgeois and feudal practices as spending too much money on weddings. If the old people are stubborn, they can be reported to local Communist officials, who will patiently persuade them to change their minds.

Young people are taught above all that their loyalty belongs to the collective: their commune, factory, or office, and, ultimately, the whole society. There is no doubt about the priority, as was indicated when the *People's Daily* attacked people who said that peasants should "love their communes as their family."

It sounded innocent enough, but not to the ears of the *People's Daily* editor, ever on the alert for the slightest heresy. He ruled that the family is a social and economic unit based on individual private ownership, and said nothing about feelings of loyalty and love. The commune, on the other hand, is a unit of collective ownership and a stage on the path from socialism to full Communism. "To a person with Communist spirit, these two kinds of love are exclusive of each other, like fire and water."

The Chinese, while stringent in their sexual outlook, are far from prudish. They treat the basic act and all its complications in a sensible, no-nonsense way. In Canton, one sultry Saturday evening, I followed a young boy and girl walking hand-in-hand through the People's Park of Culture. They led me straight into a birth-control exhibition, where for some time they studied the diagrams and devices with serious concentration and not a single snigger.

Birth control is again being frankly advocated, although not with the same sweeping enthusiasm that marked the 1956–57 campaign. That ended amid the early euphoria of the Great Leap Forward, as officials proclaimed instant industrialization and maintained that in the Communist millenium, soon to be achieved, there need be no limits on the numbers of Chinese. As the Great Leap floundered, officials adopted more sober, pragmatic policies, while again recognizing the need to check their population swell (officially, the Chinese claim a population of 700,000,000; some Western experts say it must be as much as 750,000,000 and is growing by between 2 and 2.5 percent each year).

Officials admit that birth control is making only slow progress in the countryside, where peasants have always regarded large families as a form of social security for their old age and as a guarantee that they will be sufficiently honored after their death. On every commune that I visited I found clinics disseminating instruction and contraceptives. But medical workers often told me it was an uphill battle to overcome centuries of ignorance and superstition.

Birth control has probably made more headway in the towns and cities, although in the absence of statistics and surveys it is impossible to be certain (the Chinese took some sort of census in 1964, but have never released the results). In every city I found cheap contraceptives displayed in drug stores and department stores, including most of the main devices known to the West except The Pill. I was told that abortions were easy to arrange and that the sterilization of either man or wife is actively encouraged.

Since the Chinese ideologues find it impossible to reconcile Marx and Malthus, it is seldom admitted that the main reason for the muted birth-control campaign is the need to curb population growth. In Shanghai, a city of ten million, a young official assured me that China was not, in fact, overpopulated. Its population density was much less than that of Britain and many other Western countries, and especially in the northwest there were vast tracts of wilderness that could, and would, be developed to take millions more.

"We advocate birth control because we want the people to have a better life," the official said. "We tell them that two children are ideal. Any more might hurt the mother's health. They might also lower the family's living standards. And they take up too much time. In the evenings, for instance, if you have a lot of children, it's much more difficult to settle down and study the *Works* of Chairman Mao."

Other officials deny that China imports food grains—more than six million tons annually—because the needs of the population exceed domestic food supplies. Instead, they say, it is economical for China to import wheat and export rice, which is roughly twice as expensive. Given the underdeveloped transportation system inside China, it also makes sense to ship foreign grain directly to the big northern cities. And because of wheat imports, the com-

munes can devote more acreage to cotton, their most
important cash crop.

There is some justification for all these arguments, but
only some. Rice exports are still only a fraction of wheat
imports. These imports account for more than 30 percent
of China's annual foreign purchases, taking up valuable
foreign exchange which might otherwise be devoted to
the capital equipment that China badly needs to boost her
heavy industry. Imports of chemical fertilizer take up
another large chunk of foreign exchange, and are a further indication of how the need to feed a swelling population saps the nation's economic growth. One senior official
told me frankly that while China's arable acreage could
theoretically be doubled, this would be impractical in the
foreseeable future because of the vast amount of necessary capital investment. Finally, while China works desperately to raise the yields on existing farmland—mainly
through improved irrigation and the use of more chemical
fertilizers—even in a good year these increases are largely
eaten up by the population growth, providing an insufficient surplus for industrial expansion.

In short, birth control seems a practical necessity, perhaps a desperate necessity. Yet for all the ingenuity of
Chinese officials, old habits die slowly. In the same drug
stores that sell contraceptives you can find whole counters
filled with powdered deer horn and other traditional
aphrodisiacs. On a commune outside Changchun they
proudly showed me their herd of nearly three hundred
reindeer. All the young males had their horns newly
sheared.

"For traditional Chinese medicine," the herdsman explained.

"For old Chinese men?" I suggested.

"Makes them feel strong," the herdsman agreed with a
sly grin.

.   .   .

China's new sexual code is partly moral, partly practical, in its inspiration. As revolutionaries the Communists were determined to sweep away the old feudal order which had, in fact, already started to disintegrate under the Republic. It was a matter of moral principle as well as practical politics to undermine the authority of the family and especially to emancipate the women. At the same time the Chinese leaders are True Believers, wedded to an almost Christian ethic of political salvation through hard work, good deeds, and pure thought. As such, they could only regard too much sexual freedom as a threat to the moral fiber of the State. In this aspect of their revolution, as in others, there is a classic contradiction. As so often happens, the revolutionary impulse toward greater freedom has been overtaken by the post-revolutionary need for repression and control.

By discouraging dating and early marriage, the Chinese act to check the population growth, but there is another practical aspect. China has a desperate shortage of engineers, doctors, and other professional people. Given this need, it makes good sense to encourage young people to concentrate on their studies. Although their methods are much more sweeping and totalitarian, the Chinese Communists would seem to agree with Arnold Toynbee's theory that Western civilization has progressed to its present high technological levels partly because we have caused our young people to postpone, in a highly artificial manner, the full flowering of their sexuality long past puberty and have thus prolonged the period of education.

Many young Chinese seem to honor this new sexual code. In the context of formal interviews their statements to foreigners must be regarded with skepticism. But among the young there is a great deal of genuine idealism, and I suspect that many are sincere in their determination to serve the state with all their energies. Whatever their feelings, others must find it difficult to escape the constant surveillance of zealous Party cadres and other activists, since there is little privacy in China today.

On the other hand, no foreigner can be sure what happens in the countryside, especially after dark. Even in the cities, where the supervision is stricter, I have often seen young people in flagrant offense of the official doctrines. In Shanghai, always the most bourgeois and Westernized of the Chinese cities, there are often couples mildly necking along the Bund. In the Pei Hai and other Peking parks I sometimes accidentally disturbed boys and girls lying in the thicker grass, and on warm evenings along the waterfront in Canton, there are couples in the shadows, clinging together on the benches. Foreign students at Chinese universities report that many of their Chinese friends *do* date, and that some make love. In general, it seems that officials tolerate a certain amount of romance, but interfere whenever it becomes too blatant or causes the student to neglect his studies. Even then, pregnancies among the unmarried are not uncommon. From Peking University and other colleges one occasionally receives reports of suicides. But since Chinese officials rarely concede that their stern demands ever lead to mental breakdowns, it is usually impossible to confirm these reports or to know whether the alleged suicide has resulted, to any extent, from sexual repression. But all the evidence indicates that whatever its value, moral or practical, the new puritanical code of the Chinese leaders seems to be less than totally effective.

In an important way it is misleading to speak of puritanism in China, since the Chinese version is so different from what we know in the West. Unlike the Western puritan, the Chinese are not obsessed with any sense of guilt or sin, at least in sexual matters (it has been argued that in *political* affairs the Chinese Communists have forsaken the traditional morality, based on shame, to

introduce the whole apparatus of guilt, confession, repentance, and forgiveness that is common to both the Christian and Communist ways). To the Chinese, past and
present, there is nothing sinful in the body nor is there
any need to abominate the flesh. Social rather than reli-
gious, the contemporary Chinese puritanism is far from
being entirely a Communist innovation. More traditional
than new, it has its roots in the doctrines of Confucius—
although for Confucius unchecked sexual dalliance was a
menace to the basic institution of the family; for the
Communists, it threatens the interests of the state.

Partly, then, the Chinese Communists may be reverting
to traditional values that were temporarily overshadowed
in recent years, at least in the cities, by China's contact
with the West. Complaining that he doesn't see *more*
Chinese boys and girls walking hand-in-hand or necking
in the bushes, a foreigner betrays some ignorance. For
while extramarital sex always had an important and tolerated place in Chinese life, that place was usually well
defined and restricted in order to preserve the basic family unit. Public displays of carnal affection were considered distasteful, and there was a general disgust with the
sexual emancipation of the West.

Today a Chinese Communist would sympathize with
the critical observations of Western habits made by Yuan
Tsu-chih, a Chinese traveler in Europe at the turn of the
century:

> As soon as a girl is twenty-one years old, she is
> permitted to find a husband whom she likes, and
> there are those who make many selections or trials
> before they make a match. They do not consider
> sexual relations preceding marriage as a shame.
> Beautiful young girls are seeking for males every-
> where; the hoary-headed and the widows can invite
> male companions as they like. The customs are bad to
> such a degree!

5

Turmoil in the Streets

It was nearly dusk, and a heavy drizzle was falling on the streets of Peking. Yet regardless of the dark and the damp, Chinese by the thousands were converging on the Boulevard of Eternal Peace. They marched in long columns to the beat of drums, the clash of cymbals, and the shrill of whistles. Many carried huge red banners, while others held bouquets of paper flowers and balloons. There were columns of young girls, each wearing lipstick and heavy rouge and carrying her dancing costume in a plastic bag. To keep off the rain many held umbrellas made of bamboo and oiled paper. Others wore bright-blue plastic raincoats. They knew they were in for a long wait.

This was the start of a typical Peking welcome for a distinguished foreign visitor, in this case, General Ibrahim Abboud, at that time the Sudanese head of state. It was also during my first month in China, and it was the first time I had seen the mass manipulation of Chinese crowds —with a skill and on a scale that would seem fantastic in any other country. It was an experience that often recurred during my eighteen months in China, and I never lost my initial sense of awe.

As we started our drive to the airport the General's aircraft was still an hour out of Peking, but the Boulevard of Eternal Peace was already filling on either side. The main ceremonial thoroughfare in the capital, the boulevard is six lanes wide (eight in some places), running a straight course for about fifteen miles and passing through the vast expanse of Tien An Men Square. On most days its width seems pretentious in relation to the thin traffic—a multitude of bicycles, pedicabs and pedicarts, but only a handful of cars, trucks, and buses—but on occasions like this it surges with humanity.

Preparations for the welcome had been evident the day before, as workers erected lavatories beside the sidewalks; these were now screened off with blue and gray canvas tents. White-smocked doctors and nurses were setting up first-aid stations at regular intervals and as we drove, we wove around young men with tapemeasures who were staking out the two middle lanes as a narrow passage for the official procession; other young men were taking up positions as markers, and groups of people were starting to form up along the outer lanes behind them. Nothing was being left to chance.

Some of the groups were singing, and there was a steady din of drums, cymbals, and an occasional band. Adding to the cacaphony, loudspeakers on the trees were blaring martial music. The dark sky was enlivened by hundreds of flags and banners strung across the boulevard. The general mood of the crowd seemed to be disciplined but festive. Many were clearly enjoying their outing, despite the rain and the prospect of a lengthy wait.

We arrived early at the airport: a new, beige-colored building, massive and oddly empty and lifeless in comparison with the usual clutter and clamor of its Western counterparts. There was no sign of casual travelers or sightseers, but only Chinese officials, diplomats, and journalists arriving to greet General Abboud. On the tarmac the welcoming committee had formed three sides of a large square. There was an honor guard of soldiers, sailors, and airmen, a military band, and hundreds of young girls in the vivid costumes of China's national minorities, many holding flags and paper streamers. The foreign ambassadors, standing patiently in the drizzle under black umbrellas, also had a place in line. In their dark suits they punctuated the colorful crowd like so many querulous exclamation marks.

Suddenly the Chinese leaders were among us, passing a few feet from where we stood. I was seeing for the first time tall, gray-haired Liu Shao-chi—the Chinese head of state—as well as Prime Minister Chou En-lai, Foreign Minister Chen Yi, and other top members of the government and Party. With the exception of the generals, all wore the typical high-collared tunic, usually gray or blue, severe in cut, but rather smart and neat.

Since I could have leaned out and touched any of the leaders, I was struck by the apparent lack of security, especially in comparison with the sweeping measures taken to protect heads of state and government in the West. I saw no armed guards at the airport, and on the road back to town there was only a policeman about every hundred yards, directing the stream of cars. The open road is bounded by trees and ditches for several miles, there is an unguarded bridge, and groups of peasants walked right to the edge of the pavement to watch the procession. My first impression was that the Chinese leaders had no fear of assassination and no hesitation about moving freely among their people. I still think this is largely true, but I soon came to appreciate the precautions that actually do exist. Before long, I was spotting the plainclothesmen who accompany the leaders (somehow, a cop always looks like a cop, no matter what his nationality). Like the protocol officers, these security officers know the face of every foreign resident in Peking and can easily spot an interloper (although once we smuggled a curious Swiss tourist into our journalists' band at the airport, and he came within spitting distance of both Chou En-lai and Soviet Prime Minister Alexei Kosygin).

And I also learned that no Chinese crowd through which
the leaders might pass is ever an amorphous mass. There
are always cadres at regular intervals who can be relied
upon to spot any unusual activity.

As the Chinese leaders passed us a Sudanese Airlines
Comet touched down on the runway and taxied in to
complete the square. It was now raining fairly hard, but
all formalities were observed—a cannon boomed a salute,
the band played the national anthems, General Abboud
inspected the honor guard, and small boys ran up to press
flowers on his entourage, while the young girls shouted,
sang, and waved their streamers.

While General Abboud went down the line of diplomats, I watched the Chinese leaders standing in a group.
Liu Shao-chi stood straight, stiff, and unsmiling; a somber
figure who looked very much like his reputation as a stern,
unbending ideologue. Chou En-lai was much more vivacious: his expression changed constantly under his bushy
black eyebrows, his eyes darted everywhere, and I saw
his foot keeping time with the band.

Then the official party moved off in its black limousines,
mostly Russian ZISs, but also one or two Chinese Red
Flags and a few fish-tailed American models. We rushed
to join the procession; back on the great boulevard our car
was the last to be allowed into the heart of the demonstration.

I have seen rallies and demonstrations of all sorts in
many cities of North America, Europe, and Asia, but
never anything like this. It was a Macy's Thanksgiving
Day parade, an Aldermaston March, a mass rally in
Tokyo or Jakarta—rolled into one, magnified many times,
infused with a particular Chinese character and gaiety,
laced with political purpose, and presented with triumphant precision. It was vastly impressive, and also somewhat frightening, this superlative marshaling of so many
thousands.

It was dark now, the streetlights were on, and the rain still fell. Although we were the last car, and about a mile behind the official procession, the people still cheered and shouted. Although they had been standing in the rain for at least three hours, they waved their streamers and beat their gongs. Of the slogans they shouted the most common was: "Mao Chuhse Wang Sui!"—"Long Live Chairman Mao!" (literally: "Chairman Mao, Ten Thousand Years!").

Some old Peking-hands estimated that the crowds were lining the road for five miles, three deep on either side, and that their number was something between two and three hundred thousand. By now some of the adults wore expressions that were distinctly glazed; but many, especially the young, who formed the majority, still seemed to be enjoying themselves, and there was no lack of vitality and even frenzy. Few were standing still. Some waved banners and balloons, others were dancing, some wore huge clown heads, and still others pranced in traditional lion costumes. There were giant drums, beaten by four men at a time, and there were endless clashing gongs and cymbals.

But the best was still to come. Ahead of us lay Tien An Men Square, with huge red balloons wafting high overhead. On all sides the massive Great Hall of the People and other public buildings were outlined by thousands of electric lights, and even the trees were damp clusters of colored bulbs. Suddenly we were sweeping around the square, but a square very different from its everyday huge and empty self. Now it was filled with troupes of pretty girls who danced on the glistening pavement to the clang and clatter of gong and cymbal. As the lights glittered through the raindrops, picking out the swirling yellows, pinks, and greens, Tien An Men Square became one vast kaleidoscope.

As we left the square the demonstrators began to disperse. Far from merely drifting away, they moved off as they had gathered, with military precision. In my hotel an hour later I could still hear the shouts, the singing, the whistles, and the tramp of marching feet as the last of the people returned to their homes.

This massive demonstration is only the start of the elaborate ritual which the Chinese have devised to impress their favorite guests. It is followed by glittering banquets in the Great Hall of the People at which the visitors, Chinese leaders, foreign ambassadors, correspondents, and several hundred selected Chinese guests sit down to a dinner of many courses including such delicacies as hundred-year eggs, sea slugs, fishes' stomachs, and—the most costly and complimentary dish of all—sharks' fins.

Again nothing is left to chance. If the visitor comes from a Moslem country, members of China's Moslem minorities will be present, conspicuous in their many-hued costumes. If he is a Buddhist, the light from the chandeliers will glimmer off the bald brown pates of Chinese bonzes in their saffron robes. If there are Roman Catholics in his country, then the company will include one or two Chinese bishops, rotund and amiable in their black robes with vivid crimson sashes.

Then there will be Liu Shao-chi or Chou En-lai to mount the rostrum and deliver polite words of praise for the way in which the visitor from X has brought social and economic progress to his country, coupled with a scathing swipe at the United States and other "imperialists," and concluded with a ringing declaration that the Chinese millions are standing shoulder to shoulder with the people of X and will never let them down.

No such visit is complete without a mass rally in another part of the same Great Hall of the People. As the leader from X strides on stage, he is faced by a vast auditorium and two sweeping balconies packed with ten thousand "people of all circles in Peking" and hung with huge banners proclaiming the militant friendship between China and X.

And so it continues for several days. Wherever he goes, whether to museums, factories, or communes, the visitor from X will be greeted by cheering crowds and more small girls with bouquets of flowers. Finally, before he leaves, will come the supreme accolade—a private talk with Chairman Mao. Then a tumultuous sendoff at the airport, and if the visitor touches down at any other Chinese city, thousands more will be mobilized to cheer him on his way.

It is a ritual that seldom varies. Only once in a while does a visiting president or premier receive less than the full treatment. A watered-down welcome almost always indicates certain political differences. Old Peking-hands learn to judge the political climate by the length of the demonstration on the big boulevard and the number of courses at the first banquet. Long before any open attacks appeared on him in the Chinese press, it was obvious that China was writing off Prince Souvanna Phouma, the neutralist Prime Minister of Laos, when he visited Peking in early 1963, since there were no crowds at all on the drive from the airport and at the banquet that night there were only five courses, and no sharks' fins.

Any leader would have to be more than human, and totally devoid of vanity, to remain unmoved by such a fantastic welcome. On that drive from the airport, just as he turns into the clamorous throngs along the big boulevard, the first thing he sees is a huge billboard portrait of himself, about thirty feet high, and always a skillful likeness. Five miles later, with the shouts of the masses still ringing in his ears, the last thing he notices as his car turns into the driveway of the State Guest House is another portrait, even larger than the first. And undoubtedly he is shown copies of that day's Peking newspapers, each with his picture in the top left-hand corner of the front pages and an editorial that sings his praises in fulsome terms.

Aside from the tickling of his personal vanity, it is no small matter for any leader to be so massively greeted in the capital of the world's largest nation, to be received by Mao Tse-tung, and to be told so often that so many millions are on his side. This is especially true for the leader of some small African nation who may have received, some weeks earlier, a much more perfunctory greeting at the White House or in Whitehall. In fact, many African and Asian leaders have been heard to say— privately and with apparent sincerity—that they have rarely been so deeply stirred and gratified. And as practical politicians many have added the plaintive wish that their own millions should be so amenable to such drill and discipline. Others, more naïve, seem to conclude that their welcome from the citizens of Peking is genuinely spontaneous, and are even more impressed.

In practical terms one massive aid program from the United States or the Soviet Union may count for more than a hundred such welcomes, especially since China cannot match its rivals' offers. Even its own small assistance schemes have often floundered amid difficulties and tardy deliveries. In the wake of the Vietnam conflict many African and Asian leaders have been impressed by American military might, and they have learned to be skeptical about Chinese pledges of support. All too often, they know, the Chinese *do* "stand idly by," despite their claims to the contrary. There is growing cynicism in the Afro–Asian world over Chinese diplomatic maneuvers and Chinese support for subversive movements. Despite the warm words of welcome, every nationalist leader knows that Peking is committed to the eventual overthrow of his regime by native Communists.

But such considerations often seem swept aside in the tumult of a Peking welcome. It would be foolish to underestimate the impression on their visitors, and hence the political gains, that the Chinese make from such skillful marshaling of their millions.

On October 1, 1949, Mao Tse-tung stood high above the crowds on Tien An Men, the towering, vermilion-walled gateway to the old Imperial City, and proclaimed the founding of the Chinese People's Republic. His tattered but well-drilled troops had already captured Peking with almost no bloodshed; south of the Yangtse other Communist armies were mopping up against the fleeing Nationalists; on Taiwan, Chiang Kai-shek had already begun his defiant but futile exile. All day the people of Peking flocked to Tien An Men and stared in wonder at their new leader, a tiny figure high above the Square. For long minutes old peasants stood still with bowed heads before the Gate in the belief, which was not entirely inappropriate, that a new Son of Heaven had ascended the Dragon Throne.

Since then Mao and the other Chinese leaders have returned to Tien An Men on the first of each October to re-enact the drama of that day. In the early years the citizens surged through the Square from dawn to dusk in casual tumult. Later, as they perfected their crowd-control techniques, the Communists shaped and ordered this flood of humanity into the most spectacular parade I have ever seen.

For many the preparations start weeks in advance, and if you drive through Tien An Men Square late at night, you see small formations drilling in the darkness. But there is no full-dress rehearsal, and on the day itself the whole parade falls into place with remarkable precision. To reach their places in time many must rise shortly after midnight. By dawn they have filled the side streets, sitting patiently beside their folded banners, reading newspapers and playing cards. On the sidewalks are the signs of formidable logistic support for this army of civilians: the inevitable canvas lavatories, the first-aid stations, and the carts dispensing tea and buns. Under the trees beside the Square, trucks with batteries of shortwave radios enable parade marshals to order each unit to its appointed place.

Sharp at ten o'clock, to a rumbling roar of acclaim, Mao and the other leaders step out on the balcony of Tien An Men to join their most important foreign guests. The Square below is packed with people—no disorderly mass, but well-drilled units that will later release pigeons and balloons on cue, and change positions so that they spell out slogans in huge Chinese characters. Above their heads more red balloons trail banners that proclaim China's favorite slogan, "Long Live Mao Tse-tung." Waving amiably from on high, Mao himself is only the smallest of specks, but he stands above a giant portrait of himself, staring out at lesser portraits of his revolutionary forerunners: Marx and Engels, Lenin and Stalin, and Dr. Sun Yat-sen, first President of the Chinese Republic. The portrait, like the legend, dwarfs the man.

After the band, immaculate in its white dress uniforms, plays the national anthem, loudspeakers screech with the shrill ritual oration of a Party leader, filled with proud boasts of economic progress and stern denunciations of "imperialism" and "neo-colonialism." Then the parade starts, as thousands on the side streets raise their banners and shuffle into line. For ninety minutes they surge through the Square, a hundred abreast and more than half a million strong. If there is any one theme to the massive marchpast, it is this: the unity of all the Chinese people under the Communist Party and Chairman Mao, and their steady progress toward prosperity and modern might. Huge floats portray factories and steel mills, livestock and sheaves of grain. There are units of peasants, workers, and students, and contingents of mothers wheel babies in carriages; gymnasts and acrobats make intricate patterns on their floats, and actors portray scenes from "revolutionary" plays and operas on other floats; waving bright scarves, members of minority races weave and wheel in traditional dances; thousands of swimmers, wearing nothing but their bathing suits, tramp past; Buddhist bonzes march stolidly in their brown and saffron robes, and three tiny nuns scamper to keep their place in line, loyally shouting with the rest, "Long Live Chairman Mao!" At the start and again at the end the parade is dominated by huge white plaster statues of Mao, his outstretched hand extending a benevolent, almost papal, blessing to the masses.

In recent years there has been no military marchpast. But stepping out with a precision that would do credit to a regiment of Guards, row after row of militia men and women tramp past with rifles, mortars, and machine guns. They underline the proud Chinese boast that any nation rash enough to invade the mainland would be swamped and decimated by the aroused and angry populace.

Then it is over. Thousands of balloons flutter to the heavens, and the people surge forward to the foot of Tien An Men, shouting their final paeans to Chairman Mao high above. With a final wave Mao is gone, and the crowds begin to disperse. On the side streets many collapse on top of crumpled banners, suddenly drained of all energy and excitement.

After one parade two West Germans argued over their reactions. Each admitted to a special sensitivity, remembering Hitler's Nuremberg rallies. One, who hates all totalitarian systems, said he was frightened and dismayed by this mammoth marchpast. More sympathetic to China, the other maintained there was no comparison to Hitler's demonstrations, since the Peking parade was more relaxed and less militant, had female participation and seemed to embody no special mass emotional surge along folk or mythical lines.

Yet only a people accustomed to the most intense and constant discipline could accomplish such a feat—this, I believe, is the main lesson of this impressive and incredible parade. In contrast to the earlier years there is no spontaneity. No ordinary Peking citizen can view the parade or even get anywhere near the center of the capital. Only model workers, peasants, and students are allowed to participate, and the few hundred Chinese spectators who receive invitations to the reviewing stand are selected with equal care. Blocking off the approaches, lines of cadres turn back any unauthorized persons.

But this is no dour and grim-faced marchpast of a whipped and beaten people. Much of the time, and despite the discipline, it is relaxed, good-humored, even gay. On both occasions that I attended this parade I was on the ground, beneath the Gate, very close to the surging throngs. There was no doubt about their enthusiasm. Except for the militia, which stared sternly ahead, each marcher craned his neck for a brief glimpse of Chairman Mao with an excitement sometimes bordering on hysteria.

At other times of the year the streets of the capital again fill with marching millions. These occasions are more grim, since they mark a Chinese protest against some action by an enemy, usually the United States. During my time in Peking, I saw many such massive demonstrations directed against alleged American aggression in the Congo, the Dominican Republic, and Vietnam. In each case the parade followed a well-ordered pattern, and only the slogans on the banners were slightly different.

At the time of Suez such demonstrations had a convenient focal point: the office of the British Chargé d'Affaires. When directed against the United States, there is no such

handy target. The marchers usually stream for several
miles up and down the Boulevard of Eternal Peace, past a
Tien An Men Square filled with troupes of actors, choirs,
and bands. In the case of protests over Vietnam they route
their march past the North Vietnamese Embassy, and are
solemnly reviewed by the Ambassador and his staff.

The pattern rarely changes. The march goes on for
three days, from dawn to dusk, and usually involves up to
three million people. Once again foreigners are alerted by
the early preparations: the same canvas lavatories, first-
aid stations, and, in summertime, extra teams of popsicle
vendors. Once again there is the same superb organization. At fixed times schools, offices, factories, and communes in the metropolitan area disgorge their alloted
number of demonstrators. These come by truck or bus or
on foot to the city center, march for several hours, and
then return by the same way. So practiced are the Communists in these protests that for the whole three days
there is seldom a gap or a piling-up in the marching ranks.

They tramp along under huge banners stating: "U.S.—
Hands Off X!" or "U.S.—Get Out of Y!" Many bear plac-
ards with crude cartoons of a long-nosed Lyndon Johnson
being kicked, pummelled, and generally humiliated by
the heroic peoples of X or Y (artists and students will
have stayed up all night preparing these for the march).
As loudspeakers on the trees blare forth martial songs, the
marchers shake their fists and shout anti-American slogans, taking their cue from the cadres on their flanks who
read off the slogans from pieces of paper. Scattered
throughout the parade are troupes of actors, who often
stop to put on skits. These are always the same. White-
faced and cringing, some actors portray Americans—
Uncle Sam in his stars-and-stripes hat, a frock-coated
Wall Street banker, and cigar-chomping generals. Other
actors, dressed as the heroic guerrillas of Vietnam or the
Dominican Republic or the Congo or wherever it might

be, glower and prance in righteous wrath, overcome the timorous "Americans" with nets and rifles, and lead them off with triumphant glee, while the crowds cheer and little children clap their hands with excitement.

On such occasions Hsinhua (the New China News Agency) will assure the world in many languages that "the Chinese capital is again boiling with indignation today as hundreds of thousands of people swept through the streets to continue the giant demonstration against U.S. imperialist aggression in . . ." (you pick the country; the formula never changes). Without actually telling a lie, Hsinhua *implies* that the demonstration is spontaneous and that the people have suddenly poured out of their homes in genuine and uncontrolled anger. Of course, no mention is ever made of the trucks and buses, the canvas lavatories, and all the other manifestations of the most meticulous and painstaking organization.

To state that on such occasions Peking is "boiling with indignation" is to enter the realm of higher fantasy. I have seen many aroused and angry mobs, from Paris to Jakarta, and in comparison these Peking protests, while massive and militant, are no more wrathful than a Sunday School picnic. I moved among them in a car, by bicycle, and on foot, and found the marchers relaxed and in the best of humor. For most, the fist-shaking and the slogan-shouting were clearly a routine to which they had long become accustomed. Far from foaming with anger, they were all too ready to have a laugh whenever a cadre muffed his cues, which happened fairly often. Most were young people, and I suspect that they regarded their few hours in the fresh air as a welcome break from the routine drudgery and drabness of their daily lives.

It is impossible to know, though it seems unlikely, whether the Chinese leaders really expect that the Vietnamese or Congolese guerrillas, hearing the news that millions are marching in Peking on their behalf, will be stirred to greater efforts. But the Chinese do have a fairly well-developed feeling for publicity. They know that their protest marches, however little they may alarm a foreign resident in Peking, who has seen it all before, have a way of making front-page news around the world. Above all, they give the impression that China is actively involved in the crisis. Thus they reaffirm Peking's claim to great-power status, and its determination to be heard, and heeded, on every major conflict.

Often, of course, such protests are little more than a rather pathetic attempt to hide China's inability to influence the outcome in any way. Even while millions were marching over Vietnam—an acute and bloody crisis on China's very doorstep—it was fairly clear that their "boiling indignation" would not cause the Chinese leaders to send their armies southward, and that, at least for the moment, the Chinese response would be largely limited to sound and fury.

This is one great drawback of the protests: they have diminishing returns. Like the boy who hollered "Wolf!" they are less and less credible. Over Vietnam, for instance, the Chinese clearly peaked too soon. In the spring of 1965, only a few weeks after the United States started its bombings of the North, the Chinese had their mammoth march. When the bombings continued, there was nothing more for the Chinese to do, since they had already expended their major propaganda weapon.

Yet I suspect that for the Chinese leaders these protest marches, and all other massive turnouts, have great importance in terms of *internal politics*. One of their favorite techniques is to create an atmosphere of militant struggle, thus to discipline their people through constant agitation (in this, of course, they follow the pattern of other totalitarian states). It is not only useful for the Chinese leaders to have the United States as a convenient enemy; it is

vitally necessary. Whatever their effect on the outside
world, these mammoth marches and rallies arouse the
populace, focus their attention on the goals of the regime,
stir up their patriotism, and distract them from the cares
and drawbacks of their daily lives.

At first I was alarmed and even frightened by these
clamorous crowds. It seemed that the Chinese leaders had
perfected their totalitarian techniques to an extent that
could only menace the outside world. As one who had
been raised in the traditions of Western individualism, I
found such rigid collective discipline both distasteful and
depressing, at the very least. It was only later that I came
to realize that the Chinese have always loved a crowd—
the larger and noisier, the better. And it was only when I
had mixed in several such crowds that I began to appreciate how little they were moved by the slogans that they
shouted, and how much more motivated they were by
their usual high spirits.

Yet I am convinced that most articulate and educated
Chinese are resentful and suspicious of the United States
and to a considerable extent support their government's
foreign policies. This is understandable, in view of the
lamentable American record with China and the traditional patterns of Chinese chauvinism. But on the evidence of all the marches and rallies the level of militancy
in a Chinese crowd is much lower than what the leaders
claim.

Two incidents best sum up my recollections of these
tumultuous occasions. Once I walked on foot to Tien An
Men Square for a rally against American intervention in
the Dominican Republic. It was the sort of spectacle that
looks alarming in the photographs: under huge banners
nearly a million people were shaking their fists in militant
wrath, harangued from the podium by no less a cheer-
leader than Chou En-lai. Arriving late, I was unable to

reach the press section and found myself thrust into the middle of a group of sturdy young girls, members of a factory's militia. At every pause in the speeches they took a cue from their leader and brandished their rifles to the sky. As they shouted their slogans their faces seemed contorted with the most horrible anger. In their element, Chinese photographers and television cameramen were all around them, shooting hundreds of feet of film for distribution abroad.

When they lowered their rifles, I smiled and winked at the girls. At first they tossed their pigtails and pretended not to notice, but one started to giggle, and soon all were laughing at the strange antics of the funny foreign devil. So much so that they missed the next round of slogans, much to the annoyance of the Chinese cameramen.

Then there was the time I decided to see a mass welcome for a foreign visitor, not from the vantage point of the official procession, but from the inside, as the demonstration was formed and shaped by hundreds of zealous cadres with special badges on their lapels. At first I was allowed to wander freely, as the people marched to their places in front of Tien An Men, an hour before the visitors were expected. While they waited, the cadres went among them, distributing balloons and paper streamers. On cue, and especially whenever I loomed near with my camera, whole groups would suddenly break into frenzied activity, practicing their shouts and cheers and waving their banners. In the Square itself hundreds of dancers in bright-hued costumes went through their paces, again under the direction of the ubiquitous cadres.

Most remarkable were the precautions taken to insure that no unauthorized persons, or genuinely spontaneous demonstrators, should join the crowds. Stretching across the center of the Square, about a hundred yards behind the demonstration, a long line of cadres clutched small paper flags and squatted on the pavement, forming a human barrier against intruders. Further on, a second line of cadres blocked the entrances to the Square. Sweeping through the crowds, the visitor would never notice these precautions.

With a visiting television cameraman, I walked back from the demonstrators to take some pictures of the line of cadres. There was immediate trouble. A young man sprang to his feet and rushed toward us, shaking his head, putting his hand over the camera lens, shouting, and roughly shoving us aside. His meaning was evident: we could take all the pictures we wanted of the demonstrators, but we were not allowed to show on film how carefully contrived their demonstration was.

6

Maoism
for the Millions

L eaning forward in his chair, his hands clasped between his knees, his blue tunic somewhat rumpled, the young Chinese worker with a great shock of black hair spoke in a low but earnest voice. "Most important," he concluded, "we must all study the *Works* of Chairman Mao. Then we can solve many problems in our work. Then we can raise the quantity and quality of our output."

Around the table in the dimly lit room, under portraits of Mao Tse-tung and Liu Shao-chi, fifteen men and five women, all dressed alike in blue or gray tunics, listened with solemn attention. Two were taking notes: a young girl secretary and the trade-union chairman of the workshop. Somewhat to my surprise, I was also in the room, which was in the New China Printing Works on the outskirts of Peking. After repeated requests, I was attending my first "meeting" in China.

Traveling through China, I have often seen whole shifts come off work in factories and march to their meeting, a stool in one hand, a notebook in the other. In my Peking hotel waiters and room boys paraded regularly through the bar on their way to the meeting room. Such meetings —to which many hours are devoted each week—are an important and time-consuming part of life for Chinese factory and office workers, students, artists, and intellectuals.

They are a prime means by which the Communist regime drills and disciplines its people in the approved Party doctrines, and exposes latent heresies.

There are different types of meetings, ranging downward in importance and intensity from the sessions of criticism and self-criticism at which backsliders and political deviates are ruthlessly harangued into making a full exposure of their failings. No foreigner would ever be allowed to attend a meeting at that level. I was sitting in on something more routine and undramatic: a "production meeting." While it is possible that the whole gathering was arranged and staged solely for my benefit, I strongly suspect that it was entirely genuine, simply because it was so routine and almost ritualistic, with most of the workers going through their paces in a matter-of-fact way that often verged on boredom and seemed entirely natural. As such, it was something of a revelation.

All the workers came from a Printing Works unit that turns out the weighty writings of Mao Tse-tung. Summoned to discuss Premier Chou En-lai's "state of the nation" speech to the National People's Congress, they had all studied summaries of the report and were now gathered to relate it to their own work in the coming year. Although the meeting lasted for ninety minutes, there was little real discussion and no debate or disagreement. The chairman would indicate a speaker or someone would seem to volunteer. Speaking in turn for two to seven minutes each, the workers had virtually the same message.

They had been greatly inspired by Premier Chou's report. Last year their unit had fulfilled its target ahead of time, this year they must do even better. There would be difficulties, but these could best be overcome by careful and repeated study of the *Works* of Chairman Mao (in other words, by reading more of the *Works* of Chairman

Mao, they could print more of the *Works* of Chairman Mao).

There were a few individual touches. One woman who said she had several children promised to organize her household more efficiently so that she could devote more time to reading Chairman Mao. One man told of a woman worker who kept her difficulties to herself and gave her raincoat to others on stormy days; everyone should learn from her example.

There was also some discussion of technical problems, but most of the speakers devoted themselves to repeating the slogans that fill the newspapers every day, urging each other to learn from those who are advanced, to take part in physical labor, to consolidate their experiences and make sound technical innovations, to be self-reliant, and above all—every speaker dwelt heavily on this theme—to study the *Works* of Chairman Mao. As one man exclaimed: "Chairman Mao's thinking is the moving force of *everything!*"

While their listeners smoked cigarettes and sipped tea, each of the workers spoke naturally, without embarrassment but also without animation or evident enthusiasm. It seemed to be a ritual to which they had long since become accustomed. Like Sunday Christians, they were intoning their responses in a dutiful and practiced way, and nothing in the secretary's scribbled transcript could possibly prove compromising or be used against them. At times the chairman struggled to stay awake.

Later I asked the Vice-Director of the Printing Works, Chi Yu-jung, if there was ever any argument, or real discussion. Mr. Chi replied that there was. Often there were differences of opinion when they discussed a particular plan or some technical aspect of their work. But this time was different, because they were discussing Premier Chou's report on the government's work.

But couldn't they express objections, however slight, to the government's record and policies?

Mr. Chi smiled with a sad politeness tinged with apparent pity for my ignorance. "But how could there be any different opinions on Premier Chou's report," he asked, "since it is based on the actual conditions of China?"

And that, it seemed, was that.

From his mountain base in the caves of Yenan, Mao Tsetung launched in the early 1940s the Party's first rectification campaign as a pilot project for the whole nation. It was the culmination of long years in the revolutionary wilderness, during which the Chinese Communists had perfected their methods of thought reform and political propaganda, often using captured Kuomintang soldiers as their guinea pigs. To some extent they drew on totalitarian techniques developed in the Soviet Union, but they also followed traditional patterns that were particularly Chinese. In 1949 they were ready to test their theories on all the Chinese millions.

One key concept is the importance of struggle. Mao saw a major challenge in the apathy and lethargy of his people, developed over centuries of reactionary rule and decades of foreign domination. While he had based his revolution on the peasants, he had few illusions about their political awareness, and once referred to the Chinese countryside as the "deep, stinking cesspool of Chinese reaction." Although an intellectual, he deeply distrusted the conservative traits of the Chinese scholars and their highly developed ability to pay lip-service to whatever regime was in power. China, he declared in 1949, was poor and backward; to give it modern might it was necessary to take the whole nation by the scruff of the neck, shake it hard, and keep on shaking. No backsliding could be tolerated, lest China relapse into its old, indifferent ways. Hence the need to develop—*and to maintain*—an atmosphere of militant struggle.

Mao found theoretical justification for this need. It is one of his prime points, and a major argument against the Russians, that "contradictions" exist in a society even after the Communists have seized power. These contradictions will continue throughout the whole period of socialist transformation and even, to some extent, after the Communist nirvana has been achieved. In practical terms, this means that "class struggle" must be waged in China for many decades, even centuries. Mao warns that Communism's enemies have not accepted their defeat: some are biding their time, others are actively plotting a comeback. Unless the people, under the leadership of the Party, exercise the utmost vigilance, the Revolution will be betrayed and capitalism restored. Witness, Mao adds with fervent disdain, the horrendous example of the Soviet Union, where "revisionism" runs rampant and Communist doctrines are daily watered down.

It is doubtful whether the Chinese leaders really fear a giant conspiracy against their regime on the part of anti-Communist counter-revolutionaries. In China today there is no serious challenge to the Party's authority. As far as can be judged, Chiang Kai-shek is thoroughly discredited among the masses and the chances for a Kuomintang comeback seem wildly remote, as much in political as in military terms. While many Chinese have reason to hate the Communist Party and would welcome its demise, there is no evidence of any organized opposition. Perhaps only the army could mount an effective challenge to the Party; hence the Party has always taken great pains to keep the army in line.

In the best Chinese literary tradition the leaders use heightened language to create an effect. True to their own background, they also think and write in military terms.

Thus every sector of Chinese society, from the opera stage to the "summer evening chatting ground," becomes a "battlefield" which the enemies of the Revolution seek to "occupy" and from which they must be ousted. This does not mean that an active and organized conspiracy is sending its agents to infiltrate the theaters and the tea-houses and to spread subversive doctrines. Rather, the leaders fear that their people will fall back on their old, complacent, self-seeking ways, unless all dangerous ideas are detected and overcome in an atmosphere of constant political struggle.

Yet Mao and his colleagues looked with horror on the sort of struggle that produced the Stalinist bloodbaths. This was neither their way nor the Chinese way. Like any revolutionaries, the Chinese Communists have never hesi-tated to kill an opponent, if such action seemed necessary. There was certainly something of a bloodbath in the months immediately after the final victories of 1949, as Party cadres urged the peasants to settle old scores against the landlords. Yet within the Party itself high-level purges have been relatively infrequent, and even when purged, the offender has usually kept his life and sometimes an honorific post. This is very much in the Chinese tradition, and it is officially stated that even Chiang Kai-shek would be welcomed back in Peking (provided that he confessed his errors); he would prob-ably even be given a vice-presidency.

With everyone—opponents, offenders, and potential converts—the Chinese Communists prefer to use persua-sion rather than coercion. True, in their intricate system of thought reform it can be important at a certain stage to overwhelm the subject with a sense of physical fear. But this is only one part of the process, since thought reform aims at nothing less than total conversion, a thorough remolding of the whole personality. And while their tech-niques may be modern, there is nothing new about the

Chinese Communists' aims. There is an old Chinese saying —"Submission by mouth is not nearly as desirable as submission by heart"—which is the crucial point in understanding all the techniques of political persuasion favored by the Chinese Communists: the propaganda, the thought reform, and the political campaigns. In an atmosphere of tension and struggle, through Christian-like techniques of confession, repentance, and forgiveness, the Chinese leaders seek to produce genuine converts to the cause. In their view, a man who obeys the Party through fear or merely through the desire for a quiet life is not only useless but is also a potential source of discontent. They seek nothing less than True Believers.

Since 1949 the Chinese Communists have never wavered in their basic attachment to these techniques. At different times, however, they have concentrated on different segments of the population, and at different times too they have eased or tightened the pressure, adjusting the delicate balance of persuasion and coercion. Thus the early anti-rightist campaigns were followed, in 1957, by the brief honeymoon of the One Hundred Flowers period, when criticism of the Party and its officials was openly urged. Badly shocked by the wave of protest that resulted, the Chinese leaders quickly slammed the lid of that Pandora's Box and cracked down hard on the worst offenders. After 1959, with the nation struggling to survive the double calamities of disastrous harvests and the bungled Great Leap Forward, there seemed to be a lessening of political pressures. With conditions improving after 1963, and partly because they *were* improving, the Party again took pains to tighten political control and to root out latent heresies.

During my time in China the whole nation was swept up in a series of campaigns that were grouped under the omnibus title of Socialist Education. Taken together they

aimed at strengthening the Party's control over every seg-
ment of the population, at rooting out "revisionist" and
other backsliding ideas, and at implanting in the younger
generation the puritanical, revolutionary fervor of the
aging leaders. Two groups came in for special attention—
peasants and intellectuals.

In 1964 the Chinese leaders were horrified to receive
reports of widespread corruption on the communes. They
learned that fifteen years of Communist rule had not
eliminated many of the habits and malpractices of centuries. Even worse, it was often commune directors and
other Party officials who showed the way. Hence, they
launched the Ssu Ching campaign.

At the same time the leadership took steps to guard
against any further such happenings. In the last half of
1965 another movement was slowly unfolded to set up on
every commune Associations of Poor and Lower-Middle
Peasants. With their impoverished backgrounds, these
were the peasants judged to be most politically reliable.
As outlined by senior officials the job of their new organizations was to work closely with the Party in watching
over the former landlords and other well-to-do peasants.
Some of these, it seems, had risen to positions of real
power on many communes, in spite of their suspect background, partly through their natural abilities and partly
because when the communes were hastily formed in 1958,
there were few loyal Party men with sufficient ability and
experience to administer such large groupings.

The Chinese leaders have generally regarded the peasants with deep distrust—even though the revolution was
based on their discontent—being well aware of their
conservative habits and of what Mao has called "the
spontaneous tendencies toward capitalism on the part of
small producers." The Chinese leaders have already had
to make concessions to these tendencies—most notably
after the initial setbacks on the communes, when they
once again allowed the peasants to tend tiny private plots,

to raise private livestock, and to trade the produce at rural fairs—concessions that soon added greatly to the meager food supplies. It must be galling for the leaders to realize that after all these years their revolution has taken only such tentative roots in the countryside, and in the summer of 1966, they were showing signs of preparing to deprive the peasants of their private plots.

The Chinese Communists are having their problems with intellectuals, too. In 1956 Chou En-lai told a Party conference that among the higher intellectuals (those in the arts, sciences, and professions) about 40 percent actively supported the Party and government. Another 40 percent, he said, formed an intermediate section—they gave their support, generally completed their tasks, but were not politically active. Another 10 percent were backward intellectuals who lacked political consciousness and opposed socialism. The final 10 percent were counter-revolutionaries or other "bad elements." Even if optimistic, which it probably was, this estimate presented a gloomy picture. In a nation with a desperate shortage of scientists, engineers, doctors, economists, and other professionals, even a modicum of dissatisfaction among the intellectuals could slow Chinese progress to a serious degree.

In the beginning the Communists could draw upon a sizable reservoir of good will and even respect. It has always been a tradition, as well as a virtual necessity, for Chinese intellectuals to serve the regime in power. After the follies and excesses of the Kuomintang most greeted the advent of the Communists with considerable hope, returning to China from the United States and other countries in the early years to offer their services. While few were Communists, most felt it their duty to support a strong and progressive government such as the Communists seemed to offer. This honeymoon was short-lived, as the demands for political orthodoxy increased and as the literature of the One Hundred Flowers period amply indicates. Today there is further evidence to show that the disenchantment and disgust of intellectuals were heightened by the government's bungled policies in the 1958–61 period and are still widespread. Some of this evidence comes from guarded official admissions in speeches and the newspapers. Some comes from refugees, and some from inside China itself, percolating through the barriers of control and coercion to reach the foreign community.

Facing up to this problem in a fitful way, the Communists have blown hot and cold toward the intellectuals. At times they have offered greater freedoms; more often they have sought to compel the intellectuals to honor their own political priorities. This tension is embodied in the demand that intellectuals should be both "red and expert"— the recent emphasis has fallen strongly on redness, or loyalty to the Party line. Political meetings are a favorite device to bring about such rectitude, even though intellectuals complain that these meetings cut badly into their time for research and study. In a parallel move intellectuals, and virtually everyone who works with his head rather than his hands, must spend one month each year in physical labor, usually in a factory or on a commune. In this manner the Communists seek to imbue the intellectuals with a healthy respect for hard physical work and to overcome the Chinese scholar's traditional disdain and contempt for all such sweaty activity. It is also a way of cutting the intellectuals down to size and, perhaps, of humiliating them in the eyes of the peasants.

From my own experience I suspect that this is an effective tactic, since it seems that working-class Chinese are vastly amused by the spectacle of an "intellectual" engaged in physical labor. They are certainly enthralled if that intellectual is a foreigner. The taxi drivers, most of them army veterans, who waited for calls in the parking lot at the front of my hotel had difficulty concealing their laughter whenever I sallied forth with pail and cloth to wash my car, and regarded the whole operation as extremely entertaining.

Much of the recent pressure on intellectuals reflects China's bitter quarrel with the Soviet Union. Through 1964 and 1965 a series of philosophers, historians, and artists were under systematic attack, and in each case the *People's Daily* and other newspapers would devote whole pages for days on end to the sorry scapegoat. Articles attacking his position would be written, not only by his colleagues and students, but also by peasants and factory workers whose only qualifications were political. The offender's works were always discovered to be more "revisionist" than revolutionary.

The first victim in this campaign was Yang Hsien-chen, a leading philosopher who was also a Central Committee member and former president of the Higher Party School. In the realm of dialectics he was assailed for maintaining that "two combines into one" instead of "one divides into two." Such arguments may seem somewhat abstruse to the average reader, but to the Chinese authorities Yang was preaching the heresy of class reconciliation and denying the need for struggle.

Next under fire was the well-known author Feng Ting, whose books, especially *The Communist View of Life,* had sold literally millions of copies in China and had received strong critical acclaim. As in the case of Yang, it was suddenly discovered that Feng had also been preaching class reconciliation and had even argued in favor of peaceful competition among nations, rather than all-out revolutionary struggle.

Branching into aesthetics, the critics next attacked Chou Ku-cheng, a Shanghai professor who had maintained that every artist should capture in his work "the spirit of the times." But this reasonable proposition was also condemned for ignoring the class struggle. Other literary men, including writers and movie directors, were accused of portraying "people in the middle"—for instance, young bourgeois intellectuals in the 1920s who were anti-Kuomintang but not always pro-Communist. It is wrong, the critics charged, to make heroes of such people. Writers must deal instead in the broadest of blacks and whites; their heroes and heroines must be the purest of proletarians or peasants, always overflowing with the utmost revolutionary fervor.

And so it went on—thousands of articles and millions of words, notable only for the banality of the argument and the fanaticism of the viewpoint. In these carefully controlled campaigns a newspaper will sometimes print an article in mild defense of the victim, in an apparent move to prolong discussion and give the illusion of free debate. But these exceptions are soon overwhelmed in a flood of rejoinders which restate the official line. Such trite tirades can only drive a genuine intellectual to despair, for he will also note that writings highly praised in one year can be sternly condemned in the next. In such circumstances the only prudent course is to remain as quiet as possible.

Most intellectuals are forced to expose themselves to constant risks. They must, after all, earn a living. They are also under continual pressure from Party officials who seek to cut them down to size. No intellectual is immune from these pressures, however highly placed, and no field or professional activity is ignored. In 1965 the architect Lin Lo-i was forced to print an abject self-criticism in the *People's Daily*, after he had designed hundreds of buildings and had reached the senior post of Chief Architect at the Peking Institute of Designing for Industrial Buildings. With a sickening self-debasement, Lin writes that he came from a bourgeois background, attended a missionary school, later studied in the United States, tried to stay above politics, and was never properly reformed. As a result his designs placed a "pleasing appearance" above "utility and economy" and paid too much attention to both traditional Chinese architecture and modern foreign methods. In this he ran afoul of the Party zealots who invariably favor the drabbest of designs. "In the past," wrote Lin, "I always thought that one would be able to design with ease once having thoroughly mastered old and new, Chinese and foreign, techniques. Now I realize that one can make a correct design only by listening to the Party's words."

In recent months, too, the performing arts have come in for special attention. Somewhat belatedly, it seems, the Chinese leaders realized that this was an important battle-field still not fully occupied for their own propaganda and still too open to the contamination of bourgeois ideas. Until recently it was possible to hear Western classical music in the concert hall and on the radio. Now, although China has several fine symphony orchestras, they rarely give public performances. Chinese newspapers and maga-zines concede that many people are still fascinated by the Western classics, but they print letters to show them the error of their ways.

These letters charge that Western music lulls the fight-ing spirit of the masses and leads to Soviet-style revision-ism. Writing in a Peking newspaper, a scientist said: "After enjoying Beethoven's Ninth Symphony many times I began to have strange illusions about the idea of 'univer-sal love' of bourgeois humanitarianism, which was praised in the choral section of the symphony. I asked myself: If the world is really filled with friendly love among the nations, then will the world not permanently rid itself of war and will there not be everlasting peace?" But in China today such peaceful notions are the rankest heresy, and the scientist summed up stoutly: "From now on I will certainly love ardently revolutionary songs that inspire one and fill one with courage, and abandon Western bourgeois music that leads one astray."

In the same newspaper a teacher admitted that he had been bewitched by Western music, both classical and light. "I gradually changed from an energetic, promising youth to a dreamy, languid young man. . . . I gradually became a lonely, haughty, arrogant, decadent, sentimental man who shunned contradictions and was afraid of struggle." He, too, had seen the error of his ways. He thought that while some Western works had been progressive when written, "they now have become highly reactionary things in the present great revolutionary era that sees the four seas seething and the five continents in upheaval."

Nor is the whole magnificent body of Chinese traditional culture immune from such criticism. In general terms, the official attitude was summed up by the editor of the *Kwangming Daily*, the newspaper directed at intellectuals, who wrote: "Of course, not all our cultural heritage consists of bad things, but the greater part of this heritage and even much of it is nothing but dross."

Confucius, whose ideas have dominated China through the centuries, poses a special problem, since he is too great to be ignored and too subversive to be accepted. For the time being, it seems, the authorities have struck a compromise.

This was evident when I visited Tsinan, near the philosopher's birthplace, and the capital of Shantung province. In the provincial museum, as in all other Chinese museums, the rooms were largely given over to paintings and displays which interpreted Chinese history in terms of a succession of peasant revolts, each a forerunner of the inevitable Communist triumph. At first I could find no sign of Shantung's most famous son. Finally I saw a single exhibit with a painting of the sage and an open volume of some of his recorded wisdom.

"And who is that?" I asked.

The guide, a teen-age girl in pigtails, seemed put off at being interrupted in her discourse on the downtrodden peasants, but answered my question readily through the interpreter.

"And who was Confucius?"

"A comparatively famous thinker."

My interpreter was from Peking, and I thought he might have been confused by the local dialect. Politely, I asked him to make sure he had it right. After a long bout of consultation with the girl he confirmed that Confucius was, in fact, a comparatively famous thinker.

"And why was he *comparatively* famous?"

There ensued another lengthy colloquy before I had my answer: "Although Confucius was a member of the bourgeoisie and lacked full class consciousness, he did advocate education for everyone, and this made him comparatively famous."

If they can do that to Confucius, then nothing can be sacred. From the summer of 1964, when a festival of Peking Operas on Contemporary Themes was held in the capital with great fanfare, it became evident that all Chinese culture was open to revision or rejection. It was stated that with their romantic tales of emperors and courtesans, many traditional operas were out of place in a revolutionary era. Others were less culpable and might be retained, but only after extensive rewriting had brought out a "progressive" message. In fact, by 1965, virtually the whole Peking stage had been won over for operas and plays and ballets on revolutionary themes, with the classics only performed for brief periods around May Day and National Day.

These modern works concentrate on two main themes: the heroic revolutionary struggle of the Communists against both the Japanese and the Kuomintang, and the problems and contradictions in the new socialist society. In the former case they are meant to remind Chinese of their revolutionary traditions and the miseries of their life before 1949. In the latter they punch out the Party line that everyone should live simply, work hard, avoid bourgeois temptations, and obey all Party directives.

To a Westerner these works are dreary, banal, and often

absurd. In one modern opera, *Two Sisters on a Mountain-side*, the heroine's big song was entitled "Something Has Gone Wrong with My Sister's Ideology." In one favored play the stage was dominated throughout by a huge pot of human manure which had been collected by a peasant family throughout the winter. The conflict in the play was between those family members who wanted to devote the manure to their own private plot and those who wished to present it to the commune for the benefit of all (the latter, of course, won their way).

Yet there may be some truth in the official claim that young Chinese had become bored and dissatisfied with the old classics, and wanted the theater to portray situations closer to their everyday life. In Peking and various provincial capitals I saw several modern plays and operas. In each case it was obvious that they were appealing to the audience. The audience often laughed loudly at the jokes and responded with evident interest to characters that they recognized from their own experience. The opera spectators were often engrossed by the traditional singsong duel of wits between the principals, and literally hung on every word. It seems that the authorities have taken pains to make their propaganda palatable by retaining as many old techniques as possible, including the colorful costumes (which are often more stylized than realistic), the bold acrobatics and dancing, the witty arguments and asides, and the other nuances and subtleties of classic opera.

It is evident that theater, like other arts, must always evolve or else atrophy, and it is not impossible that in future decades, when political pressures recede, Chinese theater may again startle us with its beauty and vitality. Yet for the time being it also seems that many Chinese are starved for the old classics, both Chinese and (in the case of ballet) foreign. Among the intellectuals of Peking the occasional visit of a European ballet company is an event of great excitement. For weeks in advance they scramble and intrigue to secure a ticket, and some even take the risk of standing outside the theater, pressing money on any foreigner who seems to have an extra ticket.

With movies the squeeze is also on. Many movies are released to a barrage of criticism in the press, and are attacked for showing the exploiting classes in a sympathetic light and for failing to preach the doctrine of class struggle with sufficient fervor. Even when under fire, these films are not withdrawn; they are retained instead as "negative examples," and people are urged to see them and to study their mistakes. Since these are usually the most beautifully filmed and effectively written of the Chinese movies, the theaters are almost always packed, and here, too, foreigners are approached for tickets. Because these critical broadsides are clearly contrived before the movie is released, there is a suspicion that the Chinese may deliberately build ideological faults into their films in order to educate the masses. But when I suggested this to a director at the Changchun Film Studio, one of China's largest, it was indignantly denied.

In the spring and summer of 1966, this continuing campaign against revisionist-minded intellectuals and artists was drastically broadened into what the Chinese termed a "great cultural revolution" and what the outside world called a purge. Whatever the proper designation, it quickly developed into the most sweeping rectification campaign in the Chinese Communist Party's history, with hundreds of senior officials losing their jobs. There were signs of a power struggle among rivals for the mantle of the ailing Mao Tse-tung. This, at any rate, seemed the most likely reason for the downfall of Peng Chen, the extrovert Mayor of Peking who had been fifth or sixth in the Party in terms of real power.

But it was just as significant that most of the leading

victims—including the Party's propaganda chief and his principal deputy—were concerned with education, communications, and other forms of indoctrination. To a man, and like the artists and intellectuals condemned before them, they were accused of spreading revisionist ideas, of seeking to restore capitalism, and of failing to drill and discipline the young in the Maoist brand of Communism.

It was not accidental that Chinese newspapers described the purge as the most profound and significant political struggle since 1949. For with determination and even desperation, the old guard were fighting their last campaign, one that sought to insure that only the most dogmatic young Communists would rise to power within the Party and that there would be no relaxation of stringent political and economic controls.

Aside from the larger campaigns, the Chinese authorities keep a close check on even the most humdrum of daily activities as part of their constant search for the slightest sign of bourgeois or "revisionist" tendencies. Nothing, it seems, is too trivial to merit the attention of officials, especially newspaper editors.

One Peking newspaper discovered a new subversive influence at work in China: the common joke. According to the newspaper, a comrade cracked a joke: It went something like this: "a nearsighted peasant mistook some chicken's dropping for jam and ate it. He also mistook a teapot for a hen and drove it away from the table to the floor." As related, it sounds simple, even simple-minded. But to the newspaper there are jokes and jokes, and this joke was a bad joke, "because it showed that our working-people were not able to distinguish fragrant odor from foul, and was an attempt at telling us to despise our class brothers."

Jokes, it seems, are not merely "idle chatter" but are always stamped with class viewpoint. Some jokes "savor

strongly of feudalism and capitalism in that they prettify
the exploiting classes and paint an ugly picture of the
working people. On the other hand, some other jokes are
vulgar and mean and appeal only to the baser instincts of
man."

Laughter is not forbidden, but the comrades must be
choosy. "If those who crack a joke are not discerning
enough, they may easily become the prey of others and
may unwittingly put themselves in the service of feudalism and capitalism by spreading non-proletarian thought
and becoming their sounding board."

Another newspaper, in the same endless search for
decadence, investigated scenic spots and found to its
horror "a great deal of filth left over from the old era." It
said that in beautiful Hangchow, the resort area near
Shanghai, many of the famous tombs "are the graves of
poets, scholars, and courtesans and are, therefore, of no
historical research value, serving merely the purpose of
spreading the foul odor of the reactionary ruling classes
among the visitors, and as such must be removed."

Taking up the chase, alert readers wrote in to protest
against the names given to different varieties of chrysan-
themums at a flower show—such as Old Temple in the
Setting Sun, The Soft Hand Applies the Rouge, and Dancing Madly When Drunk. The newspaper observed: "The
readers maintain that the names of these flowers are a
poison left by degenerate feudal scholars and decadent
bourgeois men of letters. In our times, the names of
flowers and flowering plants should also spread the fragrant odor of the socialist era. . . ."

Soon more readers were getting into the act, jotting
down the names of streets, shops, mountains, and even
railway stations. They came up with such examples as
Jade Emperor Mountain, Watching Fairy Bridge, Good
Deeds Done in Former Lives Lane, Many Blessings Hotel,
and, worst of all, The U.S.–Chinese Cooperative Hair-

dressing Salon. These names, they pointed out, "were obviously not in keeping with the spirit of our times and, therefore, should be changed into meaningful and healthy names."

It should now be evident that, like most revolutionaries, the Chinese Communists lack any sense of humor, in itself a most un-Chinese trait. So great is their pompous solemnity that it is often difficult to remember that behind such sober strictures there often lies a commendable determination to uproot all past injustices. It is, perhaps, a case of the baby and the bathwater. At any rate, the same lack of humor is a mark of all their propaganda.

In a speech to women ping-pong players, the champion Hsu Ying-sheng warned them that technique alone was not enough, and that to play really well they must place politics in command. He urged them especially to "exercise your minds to find out how to apply Chairman Mao's words to your table-tennis playing." Hsu failed to explain just how Chairman Mao's rather heavy theoretical writings could be related to ping-pong, but he did have one practical hint for the girls: "If we take the ball as Chiang Kai-shek's head and smash it with our bats, then how powerful will be our strokes!"

Of all the absurdities of Chinese propaganda, nothing seems so farfetched and exaggerated, at least to the foreigner, as the constant adulation of Mao Tse-tung. Piously proclaimed in every interview, shouted in slogans, sung in songs, splashed on banners and in newspaper headlines, his name seems woven into the very texture of Chinese daily life. It is certainly inescapable.

On a Saturday night in Shanghai, I attended a singing competition in a Worker's Palace of Culture. Groups from different factories were performing on an open-air basketball court before a solemn panel of judges. Entertainment was suspended for a moment as the hundreds of spectators clapped the foreign guest to his seat. Then it was resumed. Almost without exception the competitors had chosen songs of praise to Chairman Mao. There was a chorus line of eight vivacious young girls, pretty despite their baggy overalls. Each clutched a volume of the *Works* of Chairman Mao as they sang "Mao Tse-tung's Thinking Is as Bright as the Sun" ("If you ask me what I'm busy with, I'm reading Chairman Mao's writings; if you ask me what I've gained, it would be too much to say—so many ideas and so much encouragement"). Then there was a solo act, a young girl singing "Chairman Mao Is a Member of My Commune"; her encore, "Song of Chairman Mao and the Party." And this was only typical, from the morning newspapers to the evening entertainment, there is no letup to the paeans, and with such dawn-to-dusk exposure it is no wonder that another favorite ditty is called "Last Night I Dreamed of Chairman Mao."

It is a chorus in which all are expected to join. No one is immune, not even Kuo Mo-jo, the distinguished poet and historian who linked his fortunes with those of the Communists and was awarded with high government posts. With no apparent trace of irony or embarrassment, he wrote an article in the *People's Daily* which described how foreign delegates to a scientific symposium in Peking had been excited to meet Chairman Mao:

> Their heartfelt rejoicing was beyond description. One of the delegation heads said: "I have had the honor of shaking hands with Chairman Mao Tse-tung. I'll not wash my hand any more and I'll take it back home directly." Some of the other delegates suggested: "You'd better put your hand in water, and let us put our hands in the water, too, so we can share the honor." We can't help being deeply moved by their heartfelt respect and love of Comrade Mao Tse-tung.

And this drivel, not from some lowly Party hack, but from the head of the Chinese Academy of Sciences. Yet the

crackdown continued through 1966, and even Kuo was
not immune; in a notable example of self-abasement he
was forced to confess that all his millions of printed words
were worthless and should be burned.

It often seems that Mao has mounted the Dragon
Throne and that a new dynasty has been proclaimed. On
the fifteenth anniversary of the Communist victory the
Chinese presented *The East Is Red,* a mammoth song-and-
dance epic of stunning theatricality, with a cast of thousands and the most ravishing visual beauty. It opened
with these lyrics: "In the Mao Tse-tung era, the Chinese
people are happy, the land is beautiful." The title song
continued:

> The East is red from the rising sun,
> In China appears Mao Tse-tung,
> He works for the people's welfare,
> He is the people's great saviour.
>
> Chairman Mao loves the people,
> He is our guide.
> He leads us onward
> To build a new China.
>
> Beloved Chairman Mao,
> Sun in our hearts!
> Your light shines for us
> In whatever we do.
> We feel you nearby
> Wherever we go.

Above all, it is the Thought of Mao Tse-tung that
evokes the most fulsome praise. Collected in four vol-
umes, his writings are held up as the Golden Guide for all
Chinese and the moving force behind all Chinese achievements, whether it be the designing of a twelve-thousand-
ton hydraulic press or the breeding of a new strain of rice.

Time and time again, on visits to factories, managers would proudly show me "technical innovations" made on the spot by enterprising workers. Some were sophisticated, others gimcrack; but in every case, it seemed, the worker owed his success to his intense study of the *Writings*.

At the Shanghai Machine Tool Factory the director, Yu Chang-do, told me about a model worker who had wanted to improve an intricate oil-press controller, but had run into difficulties and had become obsessed with the idea of failure.

"But he read Chairman Mao's *On Practice* and then he was able to develop a controller on the highest international standards."

I said that having sampled the work in question—a rather heavy political tome—I was somewhat surprised that it had any connection with oil-press controllers, whatever their standard.

Mr. Yu shot me a glance that had some pity in it.

"You see," he said, "by reading Chairman Mao, he gained confidence and realized that failure is the mother of success. He was worried at the start, but after reading Chairman Mao he was full of confidence that he would overcome all his obstacles."

In other words, "If at first you don't succeed. . . ."

At any rate, no public speech or newspaper article is complete without its ritualistic reference to the thought of Mao Tse-tung:

"The thought of Chairman Mao is a magic wand with which the Chinese have been winning victories in revolution and construction." (Speaker at a conference of poor and lower-middle peasants in Canton)

"When you come across new words, consult the dictionary; when you come across problems, consult the *Selected Works of Mao Tse-tung*." (*China Youth Daily*)

Six hundred and fifty million people and Chairman
Mao's thinking: "these are our country's two biggest as-
sets." (Peking *People's Daily*)

China's victory in the 1965 World Table Tennis Cham-
pionship in Yugoslavia was "the result of holding high the
great red banner of Mao Tse-tung's thought . . . the
players have set an excellent example for the people of the
whole country on how to study and creatively apply Mao
Tse-tung's thought in all fields of activity." (Peking *People's Daily*)

"All those things which conform with the thought of
Mao Tse-tung are correct, and we must believe in them
and support and approve of them. All those things which
do not conform with the thought of Mao Tse-tung are
erroneous, and, despite anything which anybody, be he a
so-called 'authority' or 'master,' may say or do, we must
not believe in them but must expose, criticize, and oppose
them." (*China Youth Daily*)

"Fish can't live without water, infants can't live without
their mother, revolutionary soldiers can't do without
Chairman Mao's works." (Soldiers of the Red Ninth Company in Shenyang, as quoted by the *Workers' Daily*)

"In the past five thousand years, was there any generation as fortunate as this generation? The moisture and
sunshine of Mao Tse-tung's thinking falls on our bodies
and penetrates into our hearts." (*China Youth Daily*)

"On the drama stage, the brilliant red banners of the
thought of Mao Tse-tung on literature and art are flutter-
ing in an impressive manner." (Peking *People's Daily*)

"The thought of Mao Tse-tung is Marxism–Leninism at
its highest and most flexible point." (*Kwangming Daily*)

Then there were the coaches of the August First
Women's Basketball Team in Peking who were worried
because their rivals had discovered how to check their
fast-break offense. As related by the Peking *Evening*

News, they turned in despair to the writings of Chairman Mao, especially his famous theoretical work, *On Contradictions*.

Soon they had the answer. One coach said, "After studying Chairman Mao's work, *On Contradictions*, we have a better understanding of the law of the development of basketball playing. The present system of offense and defense, which is much improved, is developed in the process of continuous struggle between the contradictions of offense and defense."

To a foreigner, or at least a Westerner, all this seems as ludicrous as it seems distasteful. In all fairness, however, certain qualifications must be made, and we must try to see the Cult of Mao in its particular Chinese context. While Western scholars still debate Mao's originality as a Marxist philosopher, many of his works may well succeed as inspirational tracts. Stripped of its jargon, this is what the *People's Daily* meant when it praised a woman eye doctor in Tsinan, who had credited Mao's *Works* for her success in many difficult operations: "Though the writings of Chairman Mao Tse-tung provide no prescriptions for eye diseases, they arm the reader with a correct class standpoint and a working method that enables him to alter and correct his ideological approach."

In other words, while offering no real shortcut to technical proficiency, the dialectical method and the theory of contradictions may suggest a useful working approach. Many of the shorter works are simple, straightforward, almost Biblical parables that hold up noble exemplars and teach the reader to persevere in the face of adversity. They also proclaim the virtues of hard work, modesty, plain living, honesty, and self-sacrifice which the Chinese Communists seek to implant in all their people. There is something in this of Confucius' dictum, "When the common people study the Way, they are easily directed."

While it would be naïve to accept the wilder claims made on behalf of Mao's writings, it would be almost as foolish to deny them any inspirational value.

There are also sound political reasons for developing the Cult of Mao. In the context of the dispute with the Soviet Union, the Chinese propagandists have sought to build up Mao as the fifth great Marxist philosopher—after Marx himself, Engels, Lenin, and Stalin—and to denigrate Khrushchev and his successors as mediocre *parvenus*. For the Chinese, with their proud feelings of racial and cultural superiority, there must also be a certain reluctance to acknowledge themselves to be disciples of a foreign, and especially Western, creed. Hence it is necessary to claim that Mao "has enriched the treasury of Marxist–Leninist thought" and is its current greatest prophet. There is also a great determination to prove to the rest of Asia, Africa, and Latin America that Mao's political and military theories, which proved so successful in the Chinese Revolution, are just as applicable to all the developing world and are, in fact, the only way for them to solve their problems.

In terms of domestic politics the father-figure of Mao is used to evoke loyalty and discipline among all the people; in this context the Party itself would be no substitute. However distasteful it would seem in the West, it is very much in the Chinese tradition to lavish such adulation on any great leader or sage, and it should never be forgotten that this poet, philosopher, military genius, and sometime statesman *is* one of the great figures in Chinese history and a worthy successor to the mightiest of Emperors. Finally, there are again the complications of translating from the Chinese: in the original these plaudits sound much less ludicrous than they do in translation.

It is also worth noting that the prestige and authority of Mao and the Chinese Communist Party rest largely on their military and political success during the revolutionary period. By now most Chinese are aware that since

1949, Mao and his colleagues have not proved infallible in their direction of the economy and their conduct of foreign affairs. As China becomes more industrialized and enters the technological era, the Party must broaden its ideological base to encompass contemporary priorities. The adulation of Mao and the cult of his writings seem part of a conscious attempt to make Maoism relevant to all modern endeavors, and hence to strengthen the Party's political appeal. This will be especially important for the Party in the immediate aftermath of Mao's death.

To the common people of China, if not to the intellectuals, such praises may sound only natural. Mao, after all, is the man who drove out the foreigners and restored to China much of its former power, status, and self-respect. Reverence is thus evoked through patriotism and chauvinism. And there is evidence to suggest that the people blame local officials rather than Mao for the follies and mistakes of the regime, just as they often absolved the Emperors.

There are also certain limits to this cult of personality. While Mao's picture, and sometimes his statue, adorns every office and institution, there are no cities, rivers, streets, or parks named after him. In fact, in all China, only one thing bears his name: the Mao Tse-tung Locomotive. His birthday is never celebrated, and in the press there are no adulatory articles describing his daily life; the only exception is the occasional story on Mao the Swimmer, describing his past plunges among young people in the Yangtse River or the Ming Tombs Reservoir outside Peking. Like the emperors of old, Mao lives in splendid seclusion, and we are told nothing about his family or his family life.

Yet for all these qualifications, it does seem at times that the Cult of Mao has got wildly out of hand. If, in his last years, Mao is invested with all the grandeur of a Son of Heaven, this may be very much in the Chinese tradi-

tion. But it is also very much *against* the traditions of
modesty and rough equality which the Chinese Communists proclaimed in their spartan years in the revolutionary wilderness. Perhaps the most telling condemnation of
the Cult of Mao comes from Mao himself, in a report
made in 1949, just before the final Communist victories:

> Guard against arrogance. For anyone in a leading
> position, this is a matter of principle and an impor-
> tant condition for maintaining unity. Even those who
> have made no serious mistakes and have achieved
> very great success in their work should not be arro-
> gant. Celebration of the birthdays of Party leaders is
> forbidden. Naming places, streets, and enterprises
> after Party leaders is likewise forbidden. We must
> keep to our style of plain living and hard work *and
> put a stop to flattery and exaggerated praise.* (Em-
> phasis added)

Some day, perhaps, these words will be recalled by
Chinese leaders or historians seeking to place Mao in
perspective. Yet I suspect that the Cult of Mao will
survive his death for a longer period than was the case
with Stalin. Mao, after all, is the Lenin and the Stalin and
(at least in military terms) the Trotsky of the Chinese
Revolution; even more than Stalin, he dominates his nation's recent history. It will be impossible to denigrate
Mao without denigrating the Revolution itself; where
Stalin could be accused of betraying the ideals of Lenin,
Mao could only be charged with betraying himself.

For some time, too, China will be ruled by Mao's
comrades-in-arms, his fellow Long March veterans. If it
was hypocritical of Khrushchev to criticize Stalin for
policies for which he himself was partly responsible, it
would be even harder for Mao's successors to disassociate
themselves from the Maoist record. It seems likely, as we
shall see later, that revisionism will spread in China more

slowly after Mao than it did in the Soviet Union after Stalin. If they are equally dogmatic, it would not make sense for Mao's successors to attack him where his record is most vulnerable—over political repression, the Great Leap Forward, and the People's Communes. For some time, too, the new leaders will need the mantle of Mao in order to maintain their own prestige with the people.

In terms of thought reform and political propaganda Peking Prison may be considered, without too much exaggeration, as a microcosm of the whole nation. Here, at any rate, it is possible to glimpse the Communists using their favorite techniques under optimum conditions.

Power, the power of the state, shows itself discreetly at the prison, which is located on Self-Renovation Street in the southwest of the capital. I saw three armed guards in khaki uniforms outside, one toting a submachine gun. But inside the walls the warders were mixing freely with the prisoners, and I was told that none of them was ever armed. The walls themselves are only about ten feet tall, topped with five strands of electrified wire in which the current is turned on at night. There are also many adjoining rooftops. Security is just as minimal in the main cell block. There is one door of steel bars at the end of each corridor; each cell has a wooden door with large glass windows. All the windows on the outside wall have glass panes; some had wire mesh but none had bars.

Any resourceful prisoner would have no trouble in escaping. But according to the director, Chang Ching-po, an old Eighth Route Army man, in fifteen years only one prisoner tried to escape, and he had been caught just inside the gate. It seemed likely to me that inmates saw no point in breaking out, since the regimented nature of Chinese society would make their detection almost certain. But to Chang it was proof that the prison was

succeeding in its policy of treating the prisoners hu-
manely and remolding them as responsible individuals.
Great stress is laid on this policy, which combines physical labor with political education and which is applied to
both common criminals and political prisoners (Chang
preferred to call these latter "counter-revolutionaries").
The prisoners spend eight hours daily working in the
prison factories, making either cotton socks or cheap plastic goods. Each day there are also two hours of study and
often, in the evening, political meetings.

"We teach them useful skills and we teach them it is
wrong to despise physical labor and we show them how
they have harmed people so they can remold themselves,"
the director explained. "We also teach them about politics
and current events so they understand that socialism will
finally win, and that imperialism and all other reactionary
things will perish."

It looked as if the education was intensive. In the cell
block the whitewashed corridor walls were covered with
essays by the prisoners. Some were about raising production in the workshops, others attacked the Soviet leaders'
modern revisionism, and some were accounts of visits to
factories and communes. Each cell had a few books on the
shelves, most of them well-thumbed paperback editions of
Mao's *Works*.

According to Chang, the prisoners are "persuaded"
through indoctrination to reform themselves and to acquire the correct political viewpoint. Physical coercion is
downgraded as much as possible. There are incentives to
good behavior. If he works hard and studies hard, a
prisoner can have his sentence shortened. Chang said that
each year about a hundred prisoners (out of eighteen
hundred) had their terms commuted. On the other hand
prisoners are punished for bad behavior. There is no
physical punishment, but these offenders spend up to a
week in the isolation cell, about three feet by five feet,

where they read the *Works* of Chairman Mao and other "helpful" books (normally, they share a larger cell with five or six other inmates. Chang was reluctant to discuss homosexuality; he implied that there was some, but that it was not a serious problem). On rare occasions, hard cases have their sentences extended, usually by six months or a year.

As we toured the workshops I asked to meet both a common criminal and a counter-revolutionary, and these were quickly produced. The first was a tall man, forty-one years old. Closely surrounded by four officials, he recited his tale (clearly, not for the first time) with a nervous grin and in a singsong way that sounded far from spontaneous. He said that he had worked for the Kuomintang during the Revolution as some sort of judge and had sentenced two to three hundred Communists to death. For this he had received seventeen years, and had now served eight. But he was behaving well, and hoped that his sentence would be commuted.

What did he think of the Communists?

The answer was a torrent of words that seemed to last for several minutes. My interpreter summed up: "He says that all the prisoners love the Communist Party and the Chinese government. They are deeply grateful to Chairman Mao and the Party for their humanitarian treatment and for their chance to study and reform themselves."

The second prisoner was a frightened young man who looked much younger than his twenty-seven years. He had already served five years of a twelve-year sentence for grafting state funds while working in a radio factory.

Why had he stolen?

"Because of my serious bourgeois ideology. I wanted to satisfy my desire for corrupt living."

What did he think now?

"Under the guidance of the Party and Chairman Mao, I am getting rid of my bourgeois ideology."

He, too, had been surrounded by officials during our brief conversation. It was easy to doubt the sincerity of both prisoners since in hope of having their sentences commuted, they had a great incentive to parrot the approved line. Yet Chang seemed satisfied that by the time of their release most prisoners had been thoroughly remolded. He said that his staff were expert at spotting those who were merely faking a reformation. He admitted that there had been some relapses, but claimed that very few of the prisoners ever returned to crime.

It is certain that officials have considerable faith in their policy of remolding criminals through physical labor and political education. This, after all, is the program that is applied to all Chinese citizens, but it is far from clear how well the program works. To know this would require more candid conversations with both officials and inmates. It would also require the sort of statistics and research that are not available to foreigners and may not even exist.

Outside the walls there are similar difficulties in assessing the success of all the political campaigns and propaganda. But during my eighteen months in China, I came gradually to conclusions based on conversations with officials, the observations of foreigners who had known China in the earlier years of Communist rule, the observations of other foreigners who had closer contact with the Chinese people than the average correspondent or diplomat, intensive study of the newspapers, and the very rare, rather dangerous, and extremely valuable unsupervised and unauthorized conversations with individual Chinese, as well as talks with refugees in Hong Kong. Based on all these sources, the conclusions seemed inescapable.

There is no doubt that in the early years political campaigns were waged with great force and fervor, and were taken very seriously by the people. For most Chinese the campaigns were a new experience, and few knew how to react to the practiced techniques of the Communist cadres. There was also a great incentive to settle old scores, and the early drives against landlords, capitalists, and other rightists were often marked by ruthless ferocity. In the immediate aftermath of revolution everything seemed in flux, and the campaigns suited an atmosphere of purgation and rebirth. Especially on the part of intellectuals there was a reservoir of good will for the Communists and a shared determination to get on with the job of making China great again. Finally, the Korean War added a new dimension of patriotism, since opponents of the regime could be condemned as malingerers and even traitors.

All this has steadily changed. As already noted, many intellectuals have been alienated by the regime's mistakes and excesses. It is much more difficult to judge the feelings of the great mass of workers and peasants. In terms of social justice and rising living standards, most still have good reason to honor the regime for its undoubted achievements. But few can be unaware of the regime's grosser mistakes and larger lunacies, especially at the time of the bungled Great Leap Forward. While the Communists have far from forfeited the Mandate of Heaven, they have certainly lost any aura of infallibility. In brief, they have become yet another dynasty: better than most and perhaps better than *any* of their predecessors, but far from perfect in the eyes of the people.

In terms of political campaigns, and the general political climate, returning foreigners almost always note a striking change which is confirmed by longtime foreign residents. Thus my first strong impression on crossing the border seems less naïve than I had initially feared. For while there has been no real letup in political pressure, most people *are* relaxed and natural in their everyday behavior. And this, it seems, is in marked contrast to the atmosphere in the early years, and at least through the

anti-Rightist campaign of 1955 and the later withering of
the One Hundred Flowers. To the returning foreigner the
people seem much less cowed and frightened, and there is
not the same physical and visual sense of repression and
control.

This is largely because the ever adaptable Chinese has
learned to live with the campaigns. Bewildered at first, he
has come to understand the mechanics and the method-
ology, since these hardly vary from campaign to campaign. Anticipating the required response, he can often
beat the cadre at his own game, especially since there is
simply not the time to subject millions of Chinese to the
full rigors of thought reform. In this somewhat slapdash
atmosphere an insincere avowal is often accepted as sufficient. More and more the Chinese has learned to bow his
head, to parrot the necessary slogans, and to keep his own
good counsel. There is nothing startling in this—it is how
the Chinese have always survived the different demands
of different dynasties. It is no coincidence that a favorite
motif of Chinese art is the bamboo, which is elastic but
strong, which bends without breaking in the fiercest
storms, and which springs back and is straight again.

To a large extent, then, the propaganda and political
campaigns are yielding diminishing returns. All the evidence indicates that the reservoir of enthusiasm has been
badly depleted. While it is impossible to deny that great
numbers still show revolutionary fervor and genuine
idealism, there is also a growing apathy to the demands of
the regime that borders at times on cynicism. Nor is this
true only of the great masses outside the apparatus of
government and Party. Backsliding among the cadres has
long been an openly acknowledged problem. On trips
around the country, on visits to communes, schools, and
factories, I often had conversations with Chinese, including senior officials, who seemed ignorant of many campaigns that were filling the columns of the *People's Daily*

and exciting the attention of foreigners in Peking. They often showed indifference if not ignorance. In the giant factories of former Manchuria, so badly crippled by the Great Leap Forward and the cutting of Soviet aid, I strongly sensed a strange lack of conviction among many of the managers. Even allowing for the difficulties of dealing through an interpreter, they seemed baffled and bewildered and repeated slogans in a way that seemed to mirror their inner doubts.

It would be wrong to say that only seventeen years after its final victories the Revolution has run out of steam or lost all its impetus. As the next chapter will indicate, revisionism in China makes progress only slowly. It would also be callous as well as premature to rejoice over the demise of a revolutionary dream in which noble ideals and practical reforms are not entirely submerged by the needs of totalitarian tyranny. But while Communism has brought lasting changes to China, it can be said with some certainty that the Chinese people are adapting themselves to Communism as they have to many another dynasty, and are less and less stirred by the drives and demands of their latest rulers.

This is certainly true of domestic drives, but it is much less so in terms of Chinese foreign policy, especially the virulent opposition to both the United States and the Soviet Union. Here, for all its extremism, Chinese propaganda seems to evoke a genuinely popular response.

While attacks on the Soviet leaders are generally limited to the vivid but rather formal polemics of speeches and pamphlets, anti-Americanism is everywhere and inescapable. Far from confined to the massive street demonstrations, it is a daily theme in the newspapers, on the stage, in the movie houses, and the classrooms. As a Canadian, friendly to the United States although often critical of her policies, I have been sickened by the sight of little Chinese boys, not even in their teens, lobbing mock hand grenades at the gaping mouth of a wooden Lyndon Johnson or charging a similar effigy with fixed bayonets and shouts of "Sha! Sha! Sha!—Kill! Kill! Kill!"

All this is smoothly justified by the Chinese authorities. According to Mrs. Liu Tsin, director of Peking Kindergarten Number Six and an evidently kind and conscientious lady, "It is only natural to teach our children to know right from wrong and to love their friends and hate their enemies." And when I suggested that in fifteen years, when her charges were young adults, relations between China and the United States might be friendlier, and that it was therefore dangerous to implant so much anti-American feeling at such a young age, Mrs. Liu gave me the standard reply: "We tell the children that the common enemy of the peoples of the world is U.S. imperialism. But we also tell them that U.S. imperialism represents only a handful of American monopolists and militarists, and that the great American people are our friends."

This seems as false and unrealistic as the daily propaganda about past American "atrocities" in China. In a typical article the *Workers' Daily* described the history of the Peking Union Hospital, built by the United States and Britain, and later bought and financed by John D. Rockefeller. Hundreds of Chinese doctors were trained in its teaching section, the famous Peking Union Medical College.

But according to the newspaper, "this was a U.S. imperialist stronghold of cultural aggression under the signboard of 'philanthropy,' a place of crime where our countrymen were tortured by being made living objects of experiments . . . the wards and operating tables there were only one of the bloody and criminal slaughtering grounds of U.S. imperialism." The violent tone of such tirades recalls Chinese propaganda during the Boxer Rebellion, when foreign missionaries who adopted and fed starving and orphaned Chinese children were similarly accused of killing them in foul experiments.

In part, such propaganda serves a useful political purpose. Like all totalitarians, the Chinese rulers use the bogeyman of a foreign enemy to make their people militant and to take their minds off adversities at home. If the Americans did not exist, Mao Tse-tung would have had to invent them. But at the same time the propaganda has some basis in fact—the generally shoddy record of the foreign powers in China—and seems to strike a responsive chord among the people.

Proudly nationalistic, the Chinese people deeply resent their past humiliations at the hands of the United States and the European nations. Knowledgeable Chinese, including some opponents of the regime, are convinced that Peking's double-barreled campaign against the Western "imperialists" and the Soviet "revisionists" has proven popular among the Chinese people and conforms to basic prejudices and traditional feelings of superiority.

At the same time many patriotic Chinese, Communist or not, have good cause to hate and to fear the United States. By supporting the decadent and corrupt Chiang Kai-shek oligarchy, Americans convinced most Chinese that they were mainly concerned with perpetuating foreign domination of the country. Whatever the legal merits of their case the Chinese strongly believe that Taiwan is an integral part of China, and that only American occupation and the Seventh Fleet keep it from them. By long barring China from the United Nations and refusing her diplomatic recognition, the United States is seen by the Chinese as denying them their rightful place in world councils. When they look beyond their borders, the Chinese find themselves virtually encircled by a string of American military bases that reaches from Japan to Thailand, that is clearly devoted to "containing" China, and that could be used at any time for the destruction of her cities.

I am not arguing that there is no need for these bases or that China does not pose some sort of threat to Western interests in Southeast Asia and the Pacific. I am simply stating that any Chinese can hardly be blamed for concluding that the United States *is* a very real and present enemy. This is one main reason why the official line of virulent hatred does not seem as farfetched to a Chinese as it does to many Westerners. Because these feelings run so deep, they are likely to survive any immediate changes in the Communist leadership. Even if new Chinese leaders trim down their global ambitions to concentrate on developing Chinese power at home and in the immediate area, their foreign policies will continue to be militantly chauvinistic. Since hostility toward the United States is intimately linked with this chauvinism, China will be a difficult nation for Americans to live with for many years to come.

7

Yenan and After

To understand the Chinese Revolution, and to make predictions about its future course, it is necessary to seek its roots. Only in this way can we comprehend the mental makeup, the drives and fears, of the veteran revolutionaries, the men who will dominate China for at least another decade.

And so, one crisp November morning, I found myself flying in an old Ilyushin 14 above the flattop mountains of north Shensi, on my way to Yenan.

From the air it was easy to see why Mao Tse-tung had picked the place. The few buildings clustered along the river bank were dominated by the mountains, desolate and lonely. It would be hard to drive an army through those rugged slabs. Yenan: only a speck on the vast map of China, but already a hallowed name in China's modern history, encrusted with legend and charged with romantic appeal.

They came here in 1937, tattered survivors of the epic Long March who had moved the base of Communist power from the warmer south to north Shensi's crueler climate. At that time Mao, Chu Teh, Chou En-lai, and the other Communist leaders were little known in the outside world, and many who did know about them scoffed at their chances of survival. They stayed in their mountain caves for ten years, living in great personal privation and directing their threadbare armies against the Japanese invaders and Chiang Kai-shek's Nationalist troops. When a massive onslaught by 230,000 Nationalists forced them to yield Yenan in 1947, it was only a tactical retreat. Two years later Chiang was on Taiwan and the Communists were proclaiming their absolute rule over one in every four human beings.

Today Yenan yields insights into the nature of that rule, especially the ruthless, puritanical core in Mao and his closest colleagues—their stress on hard work and frugality, their morbid fear of any cravings for simple pleasures and material comforts. It was during the hard years at Yenan that this tough-minded outlook, born on the Long March, became ingrained. It was in the caves at Yenan that Mao wrote more than half of his famous pamphlets, attacking "individualism," "humanitarianism," and other bourgeois deviations.

Yenan is still a rugged place. Far off the tourist's beaten track, it receives only a few hundred visitors each year, mainly foreign delegations and leaders of China's national minorities, brought to be indoctrinated with tales of the revolution and the ever-growing myth of Mao. There are no regular flights. The Soviet-built plane leaves Sian, the capital of Shensi, whenever there is need. Dipping down amid the lonely mountains, it follows the muddy Yen River and lands on the airstrip beneath Bao Pagoda, dating from the T'ang Dynasty and the symbol of Yenan.

There is still a frontier feeling to the town. There is electricity, but the wide streets are still unpaved and lined with crude one-story buildings. Most of the thirty-nine thousand residents prefer to live in caves built on and into the mountainsides. Yet Communist officials are slowly turning Yenan into a national shrine, and it is easy to envisage the day when the present primitive inn will be expanded, and Africans and Asians will be invited by the thousands to imbibe revolutionary doctrine with the harsh mountain air.

There is a small but well-stocked museum and pretty young guides with pigtails and pink cheeks. Preserved in glass cases are the Eighth Route Army's bedraggled gray uniforms and primitive weapons, including a string of firecrackers in an empty gasoline tin that was meant to frighten the enemy by sounding like a machine gun. Most striking is the Cult of Mao that engulfs all Yenan. The museum guide brings his name into every third or fourth sentence; on every wall, in vivid gold lettering on sumptuous red silk, there are several quotations from the *Works*.

Then there are the caves. Bombed by the Japanese and pillaged by the Nationalists, they have been restored by the Communists. Strictly speaking, they are not really caves although that is the official translation. Some are separate structures of earth and stone; others are partly dug out of the hillsides, with rooms and thatched roofs built in front. There are four sets of caves, scattered around the valley, in which Mao Tse-tung lived and worked between 1937 and 1947, often keeping on the move to avoid the Japanese bombers. Spartan in their simplicity, they have stone floors, low ceilings, and whitewashed walls. Furnishings are modest: a very hard bed, a few chairs, a simple desk, a washstand, and, in one cave, Chairman Mao's wooden bath. Some of the furnishings are originals and others are reproductions; the guides scrupulously tell you which is which. The same is true of the pens, inkstands, tea mugs, and coal-oil lamps.

The young guides are quick to relate how Chairman Mao always practiced what he preached. Often he worked through the night; when leaving his desk to pace around the room in thought, he would always lower the wick of the lamp to save on fuel. Through one bitter winter after another he wore the same tattered coat and rebuked an aide who had a new one made.

It is easy to scoff at such unsophisticated homilies, which are rather in the manner of George Washington and the cherry tree. But it is clear that the harsh demands

of life in Yenan molded the leaders' outlook. After visiting
the caves, it is easier to understand the strength of the ties
that still bind the Long March veterans, and the relative
lack of high-level purges. In the museum you can view
simple paper-making devices and other crude instru-
ments, and learn how the Communist leaders proclaimed
a doctrine of economic self-sufficiency in order to beat the
Kuomintang blockade, just as twenty years later, deprived
of Soviet aid, they launched the proud drive for Self-Reliance. It is also easier to appreciate how Mao and his
ragged soldiers were able to win the loyalty and support
of millions of peasants, the support that made possible
their eventual victory over the much larger and better
equipped armies of Chiang Kai-shek.

There is, for instance, the experience of Li Yu-hua. A
wrinkled, grizzled old peasant, Li is director of the Willow Grove production brigade, part of a commune in the
hills outside Yenan. He tells his story readily to any
visitor, but it checks out with earlier chronicles of the
period and the place, and there is no reason to doubt its
authenticity. As Li tells it, he and his family fled to Yenan
from Kuomintang-held areas in 1939, with all their pos-
sessions wrapped in a single quilt. They had one more
experience with the Nationalists, in 1947, when they held
Yenan for thirteen months. According to Li they robbed
the peasants of their animals, grain, and furniture, burned
their houses, and cut down their fruit trees for firewood.

In Li's village, one of four in his brigade, the peasants
have dug their homes out of the hillside. These caves are
crowded and whole families share a single dark room. But
they are also snug, warm, and scrupulously neat. In several homes clocks, thermos flasks, electric lighting, bicycles, and privately owned pigs and chickens are evidence of growing prosperity. For the first time, Li said
proudly, everyone in the village had a pair of rubber

boots. He was just as proud of his own new cave, built in the previous winter, which had three rooms, each with its separate front door. Li, a widower, lived there with his two married sons and their families, thirteen people in all. This was early winter, and much of the cave was filled with piles of corn and vats of vegetables stored for the long months ahead; no one would go hungry.

The last of the millet and wheat had been harvested. In his tiny office the brigade accountant was adding up the work points for the year, calculating the amount of grain, vegetables, fruit, and money each peasant would receive. This had been only an ordinary year, Li said, since rain had damaged the wheat.

Cries of children drifted up the hillside. In the past, said Li, all the peasants had been illiterate. Now all the children learned to read and write in the brigade's primary school. According to the school director, 85 percent of the previous year's graduating class went on to middle school in Yenan.

There was no question of a lazy winter for the peasants. Loping up the mountainside—leaving his younger visitor panting in his wake—Li led the way to where the peasants were digging new terraces, carving lovely contours on the cold and desolate slopes. By next harvest apple trees and millet would be growing on this newly claimed land.

In such a rugged setting the "spirit of Yenan" makes sense, and the discipline, frugality, and self-sacrifice preached and practiced by the Yenan leaders appear as necessary and inevitable components of both the Communist victory and further progress in China. It is only on returning to the cities that doubt sets in. It is the young who raise the question: engineers, teachers, office workers, artists, even junior Communist Party officials. What is Yenan to them; what are they to Yenan? Not having suffered in the past, how can they possibly appre-

ciate the need for continued self-sacrifice? Like young
people in the Soviet Union, why should they not aspire to
a new wristwatch, a pair of tapered slacks, and the right
to give voice to their thoughts?

It is difficult to visit Yenan without being stirred by the
high romance of its revolutionary glories. But it is equally
difficult to imagine that the spirit of Yenan can long retain
its hold on a China that has advanced from firecrackers in
gasoline tins to nuclear arms.

And this is precisely what the Chinese leaders fear the
most. For all their clamoring, it is doubtful if they really
anticipate an invasion by the United States and the Chinese Nationalists on Taiwan. And while there may be
some internal discontent, there is no evidence that this has
reached the stage where an uprising might directly challenge the authority of the Communist regime. And yet, as
they see it, their revolution could be betrayed, not by
some sinister band of plotters but through apathy and
selfishness among the younger generation, and especially
those who are rising to positions of power within the
Party, the government, and the professions. It was this
concern, as much as any naked power struggle, that seems
to have motivated the purge or "great cultural revolution"
of 1966.

In private conversations with foreign visitors Mao
dwelt on this theme again and again; it was one of his
fundamental obsessions. He complained that the young
were soft, that they had never fought a war or been
bloodied in battle. Having never made a revolution, they
failed to appreciate the demands of the revolutionary
regime. In the view of the old leaders it will take two
hundred years or more to insure the victory of Communism in China, and these decades must be marked by
plain living, hard work, and the most relentless political
orthodoxy. By failing to understand this need, and by
demanding greater personal freedom and more creature
comforts, young people threaten to turn China down the

slippery slope of "revisionism," undermining the purity of Party dogma and leading inevitably to a "restoration of capitalism."

Newspapers are filled with articles on the need to train "revolutionary successors." It is conceded that young people have no direct knowledge of the poverty and brutality and injustice of life under the Kuomintang, and may therefore not appreciate the need for continued class struggle. It is also conceded that "to make revolution" in a socialist society is a much more humdrum, unromantic business than the actual fighting of a revolution. This is one reason why the regime seeks to maintain an atmosphere of militant struggle. In part, but only in part, it explains the daily diatribes against the United States, since the threat of an external enemy permits the regime to whip up patriotic fervor and to drill and discipline millions of young Chinese in militia units, a movement which has much more political than military significance. It also explains the startling outbursts of publicity and praise for such ordinary figures as Lei Feng, Sun Le-yi, and Wang Chieh.

A soldier and Party member, Lei Feng lived a short and simple life. At the age of twenty-two he died an accidental and unheroic death, when a truck knocked over a fencepost which crushed his skull. Too young to have fought in either the Revolution or the Korean War, Lei Feng perished without ever having fired a shot in anger. Instead, and this is the real point, his years were filled with simple good deeds. As related by the Party propagandists, these show Lei Feng to have been a sort of super Boy Scout, forever darning holes in his socks, giving his coat to old ladies, helping bricklayers on a building site, practicing grenade throwing until his fingers bled, and generally manifesting a most startling amount of hard work and self-sacrifice.

It is somewhat surprising that in the midst of all this activity Lei Feng found time to write a diary remarkable for its length (two hundred thousand words), for its banality, and for its absolute fidelity to approved Party doctrine ("There could be no me without the Communist Party"). Lei's life and diary are the subject of thousands of newspaper articles and a full-length movie. Stripped of their jargon, this is their message: so many years after the Communist victory there is no more romance in revolution. But every job, however dull and menial, serves the Revolution. To serve their country, young Chinese must emulate Lei Feng and express their heroism and devotion in simple acts of hard work and self-sacrifice. There is some doubt whether Lei Feng and his famous diary had much basis in reality, but that is hardly the point. If Lei Feng did not exist, the regime would have invented him, as is true of other noble examples who followed in his wake.

During 1965 an exhaustive press campaign drew attention to another ideal soldier, Quartermaster Sun Le-yi. Newspapers were filled with pictures of Sun reading Mao's *Works,* working through the night on his accounts in search of a one-cent error, padding the trousers of an arthritic soldier, gathering night soil, and hanging a net to protect the food from flies. Then there was a third soldier, Wang Chieh, who died at the age of twenty-three when a package of explosives was accidentally set off during training. Wang threw himself on top the explosives, thus saving the life of many comrades—the last of many acts of noble dedication according to the Party press. Wang, too, was something of a writer, although hardly in the Lei Feng class. But extracts from his hundred-thousand word diary, as published in the press, again stressed the need for young Chinese to be dedicated and loyal.

At first it is hard to understand the urgency with which the Chinese leaders express their fears about the younger generation. Foreigners, whether residents or visitors, are always struck by the militant spirit of the young people they encounter. Whether you see them working, studying, taking part in demonstrations, or engaging in such "collective spare-time activities" as hiking and swimming, young Chinese seem disciplined and devoted to an extent that is both impressive and frightening. It is impressive because it is clear that millions of young people have been stirred and aroused as almost never before in the history of China. For the first time the future of China is theirs to build, and they show confidence, self-assurance, and a great deal of genuine idealism. It is frightening because this idealism often seems blinkered and fanatic, coupled with a narrow chauvinism and an attitude to the outside world which mixes arrogance and a lack of curiosity in equal proportions.

Most young Chinese have clearly been stirred by much of the propaganda that is implanted in them from kindergarten onward. Few have direct knowledge of pre-Communist days, but they know that China, humiliated by the foreign powers within the lifetime of their parents and grandparents, has now stood up on her feet and has begun to shake the world. For this they honor the regime, and to this proud nationalism the Communists cleverly direct their appeals.

Visiting a classroom of Number Four Middle School in Peking, I found that the students had been learning English. Some of their efforts in composition were posted on the bulletin board. One carefully penned composition was called "My Dream"; it turned out that the dream of this particular Chinese teen-ager was "to serve China and grow lots of wheats." The writer had firm views on world conditions: "How happy our life is at our great motherland. But today many poor people in the capitalist countries still live very miserable life."

On the day after Nikita Khrushchev fell from power roomboys in my hotel crowded into my office when the

morning newspapers were delivered, pointing to the story
and chuckling with glee. They were pleased because
China's great enemy had been defeated, just as their
leaders had always said he would. That same evening,
after the announcement that China had just exploded her
first atomic device, waiters burst into the hotel's dining
room, waving the official broadsheet and shouting "Boom!
Boom!" It was a great day for the Chinese.

In the same vein factory managers are almost always
quick to state that Soviet machinery, delivered before the
break in 1960, has never quite measured up to the job—
or, at least, not until Chinese technicians had found ways
of correcting the faults.

To understand the depth of this pride, you have to
realize how it has grown out of the humiliation felt by
educated Chinese in the last half of the nineteenth century, when they discovered that their excellent but static
civilization, so long protected from the intrusion of Western influence, was no match for the European powers'
gunboats and other dynamic devices. The shame and
frustration were summed up rather plaintively in 1900 by
the Manchu dignitary Tun Li-chen, who drew a bitter
lesson from the "pacing horse" lantern, an elaborate Chinese toy in which the heat from a candle moved a wheel
on which were painted carts and horses:

> The "pacing horse" lamp, with its wheel which is
> controlled by a flame and its mechanism revolved by
> that wheel, is in the same class with the steamships
> and railroads of the present day. For if its (principles
> of operation) had been pushed and extended, so that
> from one abstruse principle there had been a search-
> ing further for the next abstruse principle, who
> knows but that during the last few hundred years
> there might not have been completed a mechanism of

real utility? What a pity that China has so limited
herself in the scope of her ingenuity, that for the
creations of her brain and the perfected essence of
her inventions, she has nothing better to show than a
children's toy! If we are amazed at the wonderful
powers (of Westerners) and remain content in our
stupidity, how can we say then in self-extenuation
that the flow of genius produced from the universe
should be widespread among them alone, and narrow
only among us? Is it not indeed something for which
we should be angry with ourselves?

In dealing with the young, the regime has other clear
advantages. It is in the Chinese tradition for scholars and
intellectuals to serve the dynasty in power, partly through
patriotism and partly because government service was
virtually the only means of advancement. Today, too, the
state is the only employer of skilled labor and Party
membership the only sure path to power. While Chinese
history is filled with notable and noble exceptions, Western ideals of individual dissent have seldom found much
place in traditional Chinese patterns of behavior, just as
Western-style liberal democracy proved inadequate when
it came to solving the vast problems raised by the original
revolution of 1911. There is, on the other hand, the
traditional Chinese respect for authority: only after prolonged and disastrous failures has any dynasty been
charged with forfeiting the Mandate of Heaven.

Yet there is evidence that the leaders' fears are not
misplaced. For Chinese youth *are* stirring restlessly under
the rigid demands of the Communist regime. During the
One Hundred Flowers period it was university students
who spoke up most boldly against the tyranny of Party
rule and demanded greater freedom. Amid the savage
crackdown that followed, their cries of protest were

strangled. But in recent months their voices of dissent
have again been heard—cautious, this time, and tentative,
but also unmistakable.

Almost every day through 1965 there were strange
scenes in Peking Station. With their few belongings
bundled into knapsacks, droves of teen-agers were boarding railway coaches. Waved on their way by parents who
were often wailing in distress, they were heading off for
Shensi, Ningsha, and other remote and rugged areas.
They were leaving behind their families, their friends,
their city habits, and all their hopes for a comfortable life.
Ahead of them there lay a strange and arduous future
among the peasants. This was not the regular exodus
during which young city-dwellers spend about a month
each year in physical labor in factories or on the communes. These young people were going to settle permanently in the countryside. In 1965 nearly half a million
youngsters left the Chinese cities in this way, according to
official statements.

Little was voluntary in their exodus. Having failed to
win places at university or even senior middle school, they
had been "directed" to their new posts by the Party. No
doubt it all made good practical sense, since Peking,
Shanghai, Canton, and other major cities are over-
crowded, and housing is still a key social problem. There
are too few jobs and too few places in the universities for
young people, but vast areas in the interior are under-
populated and only sparsely cultivated. By sending millions of young people to these frontier regions, the regime
hopes to ease the pressure on the cities, increase the
nation's food supplies, and, as a far from incidental bonus,
toughen the bodies of the young and temper their political
outlook through hard physical labor.

Many accept their assignments gladly, with patriotic

fervor and a sense of adventure. But anyone who saw those station farewells can testify that only part of the story is conveyed by magazine pictures of smiling, bright-eyed youths waving proudly from the platforms of the coaches. I learned of the anguish caused in one Peking family when their sixteen-year-old daughter was suddenly told that she would be leaving for Ningsha in three hours. In tearful desperation her parents appealed to a local Party official. His soothing reply: "There is nothing to worry about. The Party has now taken over your role. We will look after everything. In time we will even find a husband for your daughter. And in two or three years she'll be able to come home for a holiday."

As for the children, while many take up their assignments with genuine enthusiasm, at least some see it as the end to all their dreams. Some have written in this vein to the newspapers, complaining that to be buried in the countryside is to waste all their talents. That the newspapers print such letters indicates fairly widespread discontent.

And this is only one example. Even if they are allowed to remain in the cities, millions of young Chinese deeply resent and deplore the political pressures that are part of their everyday life: the political meetings that take up many hours each week; the ideological straitjacket that stifles pure research and free expression. They regret their loss of status, their low wages, their regular bouts of physical labor. They are not counter-revolutionaries. Most honor and support the Communists for their achievements and for their goal of making China into a strong and respected power. But after seventeen years of stringent and severe Communist discipline they feel that by relaxing political demands, the regime could free their creative energies and thus more quickly attain that goal.

There is evidence for this not only in the observations of foreign teachers and foreign students who have fairly close contact with young Chinese. As part of a campaign to expose and eradicate such heresies, even the official press has been forced to admit that such sentiments exist. Through much of 1965 the columns of *China Youth Daily* were partly filled with a lengthy discussion of the major heresy, summed up in the slogan: "To be passable politically, to be very good professionally, and to be comfortable in daily life" (like most Chinese slogans, it is less cumbersome in the original). While it may sound reasonable enough, this slogan runs counter to official demands that young scientists and intellectuals should be both "red and expert," with a strong emphasis on redness, or loyalty to the Party line. It offends against the dogma that no one should be too concerned with material comfort or personal status. In the official view, to be only "passable politically" is a dangerous doctrine because it could open the floodgates to Soviet-style revisionism, with a new elite of young and apolitical professional workers showing the way.

Yet according to *China Youth*, "this idea is embraced not only by part of the college students and teachers, but also by some young scientists, technicians, and workers in art and literature, as well as other young intellectuals." It was certainly shared by some of the young people who were permitted to publish their thoughts in the newspaper, in order to provide ammunition for a final, official rebuttal.

The "debate" was launched with a letter from Chin Jung-hsiu of the Peking Institute of Iron and Steel Technology. Significantly, this is an elite institution, and entrance is granted only to students with a good political record. Chin wrote that the old exploiting classes had been overthrown, that their remnants could do no great harm, and that scientists and intellectuals should concentrate on building the new society. They should be good at

their jobs—this was the crucial point: it was impractical
to expect them to be red as well as expert—"being red and
being expert should be two different roads leading to the
same end." If they did their jobs well, they should have a
good social position, earn good wages, and thus solve their
problem of yearning "to live a comfortable life."

Another student at the Institute, Tien Ho-shui, agreed
that whether a man should be more red or more expert
depended on his job: "for those who specialize in social
sciences and those who engage in full-time political work,
the requirement of being red should be higher. For those
who specialize in natural sciences, the requirement of
being expert should be higher, and that of being red
should be lowered to a proper extent." Even bourgeois
technicians could serve socialism, Tien wrote, adding
trenchantly: "According to my knowledge, none of the
great natural scientists in the world is well versed in
Marxism–Leninism."

To a Western observer these letters struck a rare note of
relative reason, in marked contrast to the tortured formu-
lations of the official ideologists. But the newspaper
printed many more letters that took issue with Chin and
Tien and echoed the Party line:

—a young architect said that because he neglected being
red, his designs were lavish and impractical;

—a language student at Peking Normal College warned
that college students who put on airs and eschew their
political studies would get "hopelessly bogged down in a
quagmire of material enjoyment";

—a singer with the Central Philharmonic Orchestra
reported that because she concentrated on improving her
technique and neglected politics, she ended up with a
repertoire of sentimental Western songs, instead of singing warmly about workers, peasants, and soldiers;

—a high jumper wrote that his performance at a recent

athletic meet had not been up to standard, because he had been thinking about his own personal advancement, and not about serving the people.

No one was surprised when the editor of *China Youth* ended the debate by revealing that the great majority of the many thousand letters received had attacked the idea of being only "passable politically," and added his own stern reaffirmation of the red-and-expert doctrine.

Yet for all their adherence to political orthodoxy, the Chinese leaders have been forced to permit a slight but significant relaxation in political pressures. And despite their own revolutionary tradition of hard work and plain living, they have made certain concessions in terms of material comforts. This is hardly suprising; as students of Chinese history the Communists know that no dynasty has long survived popular discontent. In the past, and however reluctantly, they have shown an ability to trim down their dogma when it threatened to have disastrous results, as when they allowed the peasants again to till their private plots and raise their private livestock.

Similar concessions have been granted to city-dwellers. Answering readers' letters—which may or may not be authentic—no less an authority than the editor of the *People's Daily* has ruled that since the state of the economy continues to improve, most people are earning more money and should be allowed to spend it more freely. Provided that people work hard and show the right political attitudes, it is all right for them to spend their salaries on brighter clothes and such expensive consumer goods as cameras; women are permitted to have permanent waves. Even the raising of goldfish—that mark of the Mandarin of old—does not necessarily manifest a bourgeois inclination, the editor stated.

As for the great mass of factory workers, office staff, and students, they must have a proper balance of rest and leisure in their lives. Everyone should have eight hours of sleep each night. Overtime is to be discouraged and to be demanded only in exceptional circumstances, when there must be proper overtime pay. There should be ample spare time for recreation and study, and most of these activities should be voluntary rather than collective. "Forcing people to take part in collective recreation and sport activities is not allowed," the *People's Daily* decreed in a major editorial.

Most remarkable of all, perhaps, are the recent rulings that political meetings should be fewer and shorter, and that what really counts is the quality of discussion, not the quantity of time. In the same editorial the *People's Daily* held that political meetings, political campaigns, and other collective activities were still necessary. "However," it added, "trouble will surely arise if a 'movement' is carried out every day and in everything, dragging the day on and on." In other words, there must be no return to the drastic demands of the Great Leap Forward, when factory and office workers were subjected to an overwhelming schedule of overtime and meetings which often drove them to the point of exhaustion, or even beyond it. It should be added, however, that this line could be easily reversed at any time, in a new surge of dogmatism. Such a reversal seemed even more possible with the apparent triumph during the 1966 political turmoil of such hard-liners as Teng Hsiao-ping, the Communist Party's tough and stocky secretary-general.

Officials also tacitly acknowledge the need for material incentives. On visits to scores of Chinese factories I have found that workers are encouraged by a wide range of bonuses and rewards. Most of these awards are made every three months and on balance it seems that at least 10 percent of the workers receive a bonus that amounts to about 10 percent of their wages for that period. Workers also benefit from their "technical innovations." Once his

innovation is adopted, the worker receives a reward
which is based on its adjudged value to the state. It
operates on a sliding scale, and a factory manager in
Tsinan gave me an example: if an innovation was worth
$5,000, the worker would get 8 to 10 percent of this. The
same manager indignantly denied that these were old-
fashioned material incentives. It was simply not true that
his workers needed any motivation other than their passion for the Communist way.

"On the one hand," he said, "these rewards show the
great concern of the state in raising the livelihood of the
workers. On the other hand, the workers themselves don't
pay too much attention to them. At the meetings each
tries to make sure that other workers get the rewards, not
himself."

With all these concessions, however, the Chinese
leaders seem to be facing up to the fact that the nation is
running out of revolutionary fervor. They seem to have
realized, however reluctantly, that people have grown
weary of the mass campaigns. While much idealism remains, it cannot motivate all the people all the time.

At first sight it might appear that the Chinese leaders
are opening the door to the revisionism they most abhor.
But on closer scrutiny this is hardly the case. So far, at
any rate, their concessions are minimal. While you can see
tighter trousers and brighter blouses, any striking indi-
viduality in appearance or behavior is still sternly condemned. With evident approval, the Peking *Evening
News* printed a reader's letter which charged indignantly
that some young men in the capital were growing side-
burns and even having their tresses blown and oiled into
waves. "They turn out looking like neither a man nor a
woman," the reader added, echoing the complaint of
many a Western parent. For days after, I roamed the
streets of Peking looking for these exotic youths. Sadly, I
found nothing quite so extreme, although it was evident

that quite a few young men and women were taking some pride in their appearance, and avoiding the plainest of proletarian trims.

While the need for material incentives is tacitly acknowledged, it is still firm policy that no professional man should earn more than about $150 to $175 a month (the average factory worker's wage is about $30), and few earn anything close to that maximum. At the Changchun Film Studio, I was told that the top actors and directors were paid about $100 a month. In Shanghai, I interviewed Dr. Chen Chung-wi, the first Chinese surgeon successfully to sew back on the severed hands and limbs of workers. Although he has been lauded in the press and at a mass rally in Peking, Dr. Chen told me that his life had been little changed by his achievements and his new status as a public hero. He used to earn $42 a month and he lived in a two-room apartment with his wife and small daughter. He still lives in the same two rooms, but he has received a pay raise—jumping two grades—and earns about $55 a month. And at the Chow Yang Hospital in Peking, I was told that doctors from the old society sometimes earn $150 a month. "This is a special policy of the state so they can maintain their original standard of living," the Deputy Director explained. But young doctors average only about $50 a month, as part of a policy "to extinguish discrepancies between workingpeople and intellectuals."*

* To put such salaries in perspective, it should be remembered that basic living costs are correspondingly low. An average factory worker earning $30 a month would pay only about $2 in rent for a two-room apartment and could buy a pair of work trousers for about $3. His wife, who would also work and earn nearly as much as he, could buy vegetables in the market for five to ten cents a pound, and pork, beef, and poultry for forty or fifty cents a pound. Medical care would be free for working members of the family and available at half-cost to their dependents.

And while there may be fewer political meetings, they still take place and there is no letup in the demands for political orthodoxy. When I visited Yunnan University in Kunming, it was the first week of spring term and the cherry blossoms were in full bloom. But the beautiful campus was strangely empty. It turned out that the students, all nineteen hundred of them, were starting the term by attending a political meeting. They were crowded into the assembly hall and overflowing on the grass outside. As we looked in, a young girl was speaking of the need for students to be "revolutionary successors," loyal and hard-working followers of the Communist cause. According to a university official, 20 to 25 percent of the lecture time was devoted to political education and current affairs. Aside from these formal lectures, he said, the students also held political discussions in their spare time on a "voluntary" basis.

Most officials explain this emphasis on political education in long-winded and jargon-infested diatribes which are filled with ritualistic references to "serving the masses" and "following the teachings of Chairman Mao." I was grateful for the more direct approach of the administrative director of Peking University. We had been discussing this question of indoctrination through an interpreter who was not quite adequate to the task. As I watched the director listen to the interpreter's English, it was quite clear that he had a better grasp of the language and was squirming at the way in which his meaning was not getting through. Suddenly, when he could take it no longer, he burst into perfect English. "We want no beatniks in China!" he exclaimed, and literally sighed with relief when he saw I understood. As for the interpreter, this young man's puzzled look clearly indicated that beatniks were not part of the approved vocabulary at his language school.

Finally, while they may now be placing less emphasis

on mass campaigns, the Chinese leaders seem to be strengthening and expanding the *institutions* of political control. In the countryside the Poor and Lower-Middle Peasants Associations are one example of this trend. In the towns and cities new political departments in key industries are another. Everywhere the Young Pioneers and the Young Communist League have been expanded and reorganized to draw all Chinese youth under their influence. Entry of freshman classes to the universities and senior middle schools was delayed for six months in 1966, pending radical changes in the selection of students and the curriculum to make sure that more youngsters from worker and peasant families were admitted and that their tuition was even more rigorously Maoist. No aspect of life is safe from Party demands: in the theater as in sports it is always a case of "putting politics in command." And, it need hardly be added, only one sort of politics is tolerated: the politics of the Chinese Communist Party.

At the root of all this activity there lies a desperate drive to maintain the purity of the Party and its cadres, the purity of the Revolution itself. Like all True Believers, the Chinese leaders are horrified by the slightest sign of corruption, whether material or ideological. Practical politicians and students of history, they know that every previous Chinese dynasty has eventually succumbed to the decadence and self-seeking of its ruling clique. Militant Communists, determined that their doctrines should conquer the world, they have the horrendous example of the Soviet Union, grown soft and lax, turning inward on itself, betraying the principles of Lenin. The specter of revisionism in all its aspects will haunt their domains for generations to come—or such is their concern.

The Chinese are especially sensitive to suggestions by American leaders that U.S.-Chinese relations might improve if the next generation of Chinese leaders adopts more moderate policies. They have scornfully rejected these suggestions, but a foreigner working in Peking as a translator gave me evidence of their concern when he told me that the present rulers demand instant translations of all such speeches and articles.

This concern antedates the Chinese quarrel with the Russians. From Yenan, in the early 1940s, Mao Tse-tung launched the Party's first rectification campaign, to purify the cadres. Shortly after winning power the Party was rooting out officials who furthered their desire for the soft life by engaging in bribery and the misuse of public funds. In 1957, during the One Hundred Flowers outburst, the Party was widely criticized for giving special privileges to its members. According to the army's secret Work Papers, which reached the West, in 1961 Peking was again very much concerned with corrupt and tyrannical cadres, just as in 1964 the leaders discovered similar tendencies on the communes.

In one of their most revealing polemics against Moscow, the Chinese argued that the "revisionism" running rampant in the Soviet Union was not entirely foreign to the local scene. While the editorial in the *People's Daily* praised the revolutionary solidarity of the masses and maintained that it would be very difficult to restore capitalism in China, it added:

> But let us look at the facts. Is our society today thoroughly clean? No, it is not. Classes and class struggle still remain, the activities of the overthrown reactionary classes plotting a comeback still continue, and we still have speculative activities by old and new bourgeois elements and desperate forays by embezzlers, grafters, and degenerates. There are also cases of degeneration in a few primary organizations; what is more, these degenerates do their utmost to find protectors and agents in the higher leading bodies. We should not in the least slacken our vigi-

lance against such phenomena but must keep fully alert.

It seems that the possibility of revisionists reaching the top in China is at least considered by the present leaders. At any rate the *People's Daily* disclosed in late 1965 that Mao Tse-tung had told delegates from other Communist Parties that "if China's leadership is usurped by revisionists in the future, the Marxist–Leninists of all countries should likewise resolutely expose and fight them, and help the working class and masses of China to combat such revisionism."

Foreign visitors find it hard to understand this concern. Each is rightly struck by the apparent honesty and rectitude of the Chinese citizenry. It has been often told how tourists can safely leave loose money in their hotel rooms, and there is no shortage of tales about tourists who tried to throw out an old handkerchief or a pair of boots, only to be pursued throughout the land by grinning guides anxious to return the precious goods. These stories are quite true, and they indicate a fetish for honesty that would seem far-fetched and absurd were it not for the commendable Chinese determination to outlive their reputation for corruption.

Great efforts are made to impress the foreigner with this new morality. In Shanghai's vast San Tao De Market, which I toured at dawn, the manager pointed with pride to a complaints desk where customers could check prices and have their purchases reweighed. As we passed, a large duck was sitting on the scales with an expression of outraged dignity, while a determined little old lady carefully checked its weight.

In the old days, the manager said, there had been private stalls in the market, and a great deal of cheating, quarreling, and even fighting. Now, I gathered, there was nothing but scrupulous honesty and friendly smiles. Well

192 [REPORTER IN RED CHINA

—almost. As we turned down one aisle, we suddenly came upon two gray-haired grannies, squabbling furiously over the contents of a shopping basket. But the manager and his assistants quickly hurried me away from the most unsocialist scene.

The foreign resident has a greater chance to realize that there actually is some dishonesty. On rare occasions I have been approached by Chinese anxious to purchase foreign cigarettes. I have even seen one or two beggars. And it is well known in Peking that a small number of foreign embassies have officers who have little trouble finding black markets for transistor radios, watches, and other contraband. But these are exceptional cases. There is nothing like the dishonesty and hooliganism that are reported to be prevalent in Soviet cities. To give only one example: I seldom locked my car in Peking; in Moscow, according to the dispatches of Western correspondents, they even lift your windshield wipers. In general, I suspect, corruption is minimal, and the old Chinese habits of "squeeze" are still largely curbed, if not entirely eliminated.

But the leaders in China must also struggle against *political* corruption: the corruption of power. More than the activities of a relatively few grafters and embezzlers, this poses a serious threat to the purity of their revolution. It demands a constant struggle to prevent the formation of any elite that might threaten the political supremacy of the Party or else erode its revolutionary dogmas.

In *The New Class* the former Yugoslav leader Milovan Djilas has argued that by concentrating all political and economic power into the hands of the Party, a Communist state inevitably creates privileges and parasitic functions, leading to its own corruption. This happens through the instrument of a New Class, or political bureaucracy, which arises *within* the revolutionary Party, erodes its idealism and initiative, and creates an oligarchy of careerists and power-seekers.

The party makes the class, but the class grows as a result and uses the party as a basis. The class grows stronger, while the party grows weaker; this is the inescapable fate of every Communist party in power.

Whether or not they have read Djilas (and they almost certainly have), the Chinese leaders are well aware of the danger. It is intensified by certain Chinese traditions, especially that whereby scholars and intellectuals serving the regime formed a special privileged elite. Thus cadres and intellectuals must do regular physical labor to overcome their traditional disdain for soiling their hands. It is also the major political reason (there are other practical ones) why the whole Chinese educational system is being converted to a part-work, part-study basis. Eventually, it is stated, virtually every Chinese school and college will be run along these lines, with the students spending half their time in the classrooms and the other half in the fields or the workshops, in order to break down the distinctions between town and country, and between mental and manual labor, and to facilitate the building of Communism. This concern also explains the fury with which the leaders attack the heresy "to be passable politically, to be very good professionally, and to be comfortable in daily life"—since this could lead to the formation of a privileged professional elite that would become increasingly remote from the political demands of the Party, and a potential basis for anti-Party activities. No one, however talented or highly placed, must be allowed to feel that he is in any sort of special position. As one Chinese official told me, with evident passion and sincerity, "Before, China was a plate of sand. Now, we must be disciplined and organized to bind our country together and to make it a unified, modern power."

Special problems are posed by the People's Liberation Army. Under previous dynasties intellectuals and bourgeoisie used to look down on military service as beneath

the dignity of their families. But in the modern era the
PLA has gained almost as much prestige as the Party
itself, with its victories against the Japanese, the Kuomintang, and in Korea. With its experienced leaders, its
weapons, and its more than two and a half million men,
the army is the Party's only serious potential rival.

The Party has blown hot and cold toward the Army, at
times bolstering its prestige and privileges, at times cutting it down to size. Steps have recently been taken which
were clearly aimed at strengthening Party control over
the PLA and preventing the development of any professional elite, less concerned with political dogma than with
new weapons and military efficiency. As was more or less
admitted at the time, this was why the soldiers were
stripped of their ranks and insignia of rank in the summer
of 1965. No longer were there any generals, colonels,
majors, or other officers; instead, all became known by
their function (Comrade Company Commander Yang,
Comrade Squad Leader Chou, and so on). And everyone
was now dressed alike in the same floppy khaki uniforms
and pudding-shaped caps, with only a single red star on
the cap and a red flag on each collar. In fact, rank and
insignia had been introduced only after the Korean War,
at the urging of the Russians, and newspaper articles
praised this return to the democratic traditions of the
PLA.

Not all the former officers seemed so enthusiastic. A few
days after the new regulations came into force some
former officers met in my hotel with a visiting delegation
of army officers from Indonesia. The Indonesians were
extremely dapper in their dark green, American-style uniforms, covered with braid and flashes. The Chinese, of
course, were all dressed the same, without any markings.
Since it was a hot day, they had taken off their caps and
jackets and left them on a coat rack outside the meeting
room. As I walked by, the meeting was breaking up. With

no insignia to guide them, the Chinese "officers" were
frantically trying on each other's caps and jackets. Here, a
Chinese would put on a cap that sank down to his nose;
there, another would have the cuffs on a jacket barely
reaching past his elbows. It was pure slapstick: they
switched and sweated with frantic embarrassment, a
scene from an old silent movie. At that moment I would
have dearly loved to have taken a poll on their opinion of
the new changes.

A few days later a handsome young soldier visited a
photography shop on the Wang Fu Ching with his wife or
girl friend. Before they posed together for the camera he
opened a plastic bag and put on his old cap and jacket,
complete with insignia, epaulettes, and ribbons. Whatever
the Party might order, his children would always have a
picture of their father in all his former glory.

The signs of privilege and prerogative often seem
equally innocent. On any Sunday in Peking you can see
senior cadres taking their families to the Great Wall or the
temples in the Western Hills in big black Zims or Buicks
or other official limousines. At the resort of Pei Tai Ho
foreigners in their compound can gaze over the fence and
view Chinese officials basking in front of their villas and
enjoying the rare pleasure of a seaside holiday. For Party
members there are other useful privileges: they can often
marry before the approved age, and have priority in
securing new apartments. Their rations of rice and cotton
cloth tend to be generous. And there are stories, apparently authentic, which tell how children of senior Party
members can avoid an assignment in the countryside by
winning a place in college to which their marks do not
always entitle them.

Then there are the more serious acts of corruption—
such as those which touched off the cleanup campaign on
the communes, and those to which the *People's Daily*
polemic against the Russians, quoted above, makes tanta-

lizing allusions. But seventeen years after the Communist victory it is perhaps surprising that there are not *more* signs of degeneration, both material and ideological; it is even more surprising, given the old Chinese tolerance of squeeze and other attendant practices. According to the Djilas doctrine, the Chinese Communist Party must inevitably generate its own corruption. While this may be inevitable, it seems to be a very slow process, and it is remarkable just how much the Yenan spirit of plain living and hard work still seems to dominate the Party.

In their twilight years the old revolutionaries in Peking are determined to implant this spirit among their successors. While reluctantly permitting certain small freedoms to both peasants and city-dwellers, they maintain that through class struggle, socialist education, and the most rigid Party control, China can be kept free of corruption, careerism, and all other aspects of revisionism. While this seems unlikely in the long run, it seems just as unlikely that the next generation of leaders will open up the floodgates to revisionism or any liberal reform.

In the Soviet Union, as Djilas has pointed out, Lenin's *revolutionary* Communism was replaced by Stalin's *dogmatic* Communism, which in turn was followed by the *non-dogmatic* Communism of Khrushchev and his successors. In China the parallels are not exact, since Mao and his contemporaries combine both the Lenin and the Stalin roles, being both revolutionaries and dogmatic purists. Further, there is little reason to suppose that after less than two decades of Communist rule dogmatism has run its course in China. Not much of any substance is known about the next generation of leaders, the men in their forties and fifties. But the ones I have met—provincial and civic officials, and Party cadres in the government ministries, the communes, and the factories—have generally seemed narrow and fanatic in their outlook.

It often seems that the old leaders in Peking are worried

that the young cadres are *too* dogmatic and make too many demands on the people. This was clearly the case when Peking issued its instructions for a slight relaxation in the daily pressures on city-dwellers. Running through them all was a concern that the purists were pushing too hard. As *China Youth Daily* complained, "We constantly run into a problem like this: some of the student cadres, being exceedingly enthusiastic, always want to arrange more activities, believing that the more activities are arranged, the brisker their work seems to be."

There was similar trouble with the campaign to have young city-dwellers settle permanently in the country-side. Here again it seemed to be a case of zealous young cadres and activists pushing a campaign too hard, evoking an atmosphere in which few dared to suggest that their talents might entitle them to further education. Newspapers printed letters in which students asked for guid-ance, stating that they wanted to take the college entrance examinations and were being urged by their friends not to bother, but to join the patriotic surge to the countryside. With evident alarm, *China Youth Daily* ruled that this was going much too far. In a clear directive to the cadres the newspaper pointed out that China needs scientists and other specialists, and that students should not be blamed for seeking a higher education: "We should not object to their studying hard, still less should we criticize them as if studying hard were a mistake."

Such evidence points to a frightening amount of narrow zealotry among the younger officials. With even less knowledge of the outside world than the present leader-ship, and without direct experience of the give-and-take of revolutionary activity, they could prove to be even more blinkered and dogmatic. Lacking the charisma of Mao and the other first-generation revolutionaries, they may find it necessary to make certain concessions in order to consolidate their power. But it seems just as likely that they will seek to maintain their position by demanding the most rigid political orthodoxy, perhaps even tightening some of the screws. It is probably significant, and hardly heartening, that recent government promotions have generally favored men attached to the military, the police, and the propaganda apparatus, rather than the more "reasonable" men associated with the conduct of the economy, trade, and foreign affairs.

The future holds a terrible dilemma for the Chinese Communist Party. Eventually they must face up to the problem that the Soviet Union is now fitfully trying to solve. To achieve modern greatness, and even to keep pace with the rate of advance in the West, the Chinese Communists must give their most talented young people some reason to perform at their highest level. By now it is evident that patriotism and Mao's *Works* are insufficient goads. But there is also little evidence that the Chinese leaders are prepared to acknowledge the need for a much more thoroughgoing system of rewards and incentives, since to make this admission is to embrace the "revisionism" they so strongly condemn.

While there is no immediate threat from an organized opposition in political terms, there are the lessons of history. Having won power, the Communists must show themselves worthy of retaining that power. To this end, armed might and ruthless suppression have never proved sufficient. It is not a question of Western-style democracy, so foreign to Chinese traditions. But to retain the Mandate of Heaven the Communists must impress the people with continued economic progress and basic social justice. Their achievements in these fields—already significant, for all the mistakes and setbacks—must be enlarged.

Yet every previous dynasty has eventually failed in these aspects and has forfeited the Mandate. Tyranny and corruption and plain lassitude have brought about their doom. For the Communists, as they themselves admit,

there is a desperate necessity to retain the original idealism and revolutionary fervor. If the energies of the Party
leaders become largely directed toward maintaining their
own powers and prerogatives, then everything is lost. This
is the crux of their dilemma: to secure their goals they
demand that the Party remain the source of all power; yet
corruption seems inevitable *because* all power and prop-
erty are vested in the Party, without any checks or bal-
ances. In his study of European Communism, Djilas has
posed the problem that faces the Chinese:

> The world has seen few heroes as ready to sacrifice
> and suffer as the Communists were on the eve of and
> during the revolution. It has probably never seen
> such characterless wretches and stupid defenders of
> arid formulas as they become after attaining power.

There are parallels in Chinese, as well as Communist,
history. If the Party turns itself into a dogmatic, self-
seeking oligarchy, then its rise and fall will parallel that of
the Chin Dynasty, as described by the Han poet and
statesman Chia I:

> Chin, beginning with an insignificant amount of terri-
> tory, reached the power of a great state and for a
> hundred years made all the other great lords pay
> homage to it. Yet after it had become master of the
> whole empire and established itself within the fast-
> ness of the Pass, a single commoner opposed it and its
> ancestral temples toppled, its ruler died by the hands
> of men, and it became the laughingstock of the
> world. Why? Because it failed to rule with humanity
> and righteousness and to realize that the power to
> attack and the power to retain what one has thereby
> won are not the same.

It can be argued that in our modern technological age,
the lessons of history are not always valid. It can be

further maintained that in their short time the Communists have so changed the face of China that parallels with the past are often misleading. Yet there is another quotation, much closer to the present day, which shows that the Communists *do* face this traditional Chinese dilemma, partly *because* their reforms have changed the face of China and unleashed new energies and demands.

In May, 1957, Miss Lin Hsi-ling, a twenty-one-year-old student at Peking University, that honored home of Chinese intellectual dissent, made a speech at the height of the One Hundred Flowers period. Extracts were later printed in a pamphlet called "Look, What Kind of Talk Is This?", prepared by the Party for its counter-attack against its critics. She said:

> We don't think it sufficient for the Party merely to employ methods of rectification, adopt reformist methods, and make minor concessions to the people. After some study, I have come to believe that all ruling classes in history have one thing in common: their democracy has limits. The democracy of the Communist Party has limits, too. During the tempest of the Revolution, Party members stayed together with the people; but after the victory of the Revolution, they climbed up to the ruling position and ideological limits were imposed. They want to suppress the people; they adopt policies aimed at deceiving the people. Actually, this is the most foolish of methods. . . .
>
> We youth have brains, but for what purpose? To let others lead us around by the nose? We want to speak up!

Lin Hsi-ling has not been heard from since. But her brave words still strike home.

8

Farewell to Peking

Winter in Peking, and the wind rages down from the Gobi Desert, blowing yellow clouds of dust and grit. At times it is almost impossible to drive along the Boulevard of Eternal Peace, enveloped by the sudden sandstorms. These part to reveal an old Chinese, bending nearly double in the wind which lashes at his tattered jacket, and whipping on a bedraggled team of horse and donkey, stolidly pulling a cart piled high with coal. Another gust and they disappear again, with only the driver's thin, high-pitched curses ringing eerily from the wilderness of floating desert.

Minutes later, and the dust has settled. For it is true, as the Communists claim, that thousands of trees, planted in the suburbs, have done much to hold the soil and break the storms. However fierce, these are nothing like the day-long blows recorded by residents of old. Soon a blue sky makes less gloomy the dun-colored hutungs, and a thin sun turns the roofs and towers of the Forbidden City into a shimmering sea of gold.

But for all the random beauty, winter in Peking is still a taut, electric time. Dust blows relentlessly through doors and windows, settling on clothes, books, tables. On the streets it clogs the throat and nostrils and seems to pene-

204 [REPORTER IN RED CHINA

trate through every pore. It is a time when nerves stretch
tight and every handshake is a duel of sparks.

For the foreign community it is a time of flaring
tempers, sudden jealousies, and bouts of deep despair. At
parties and receptions it is always the same few faces, the
same old gossip, the same tired tirades against Them, the
Chinese officials, who seem almost to have invented this
cruel season in order to break our wills. And outside on
the streets, depressingly alike in their cotton-padded
coats, the citizens of Peking trundle on their rounds, a
blue-clad army from which we must always remain remote.

It is a time for recalling old affairs, absent lovers,
warmer climes. It is a time when many begin to hate the
choice or chance that brought them to Peking. Above all,
it is a time to feel the vast indifference of China toward
the foreigner.

After one year in China, I too suffered this malaise, this
enervation of will and interest. No longer could I find
much amusement in the larger lunacies of Chinese propaganda, my daily working fare. No longer could I enjoy the
small victories sometimes won over Chinese officialdom or
the tortured formality of our exchanges. No longer was I
reassured by the sights and sounds and smells of the
Peking streets, finding consolation in the sly roguery of
the pedicab drivers or beauty in the wise faces of the
ancient grannies.

It was more than a case of losing sympathy for the
place and the people, and none of it was China's fault. Like
thousands of foreigners before me, I was finding out how
life in China can test the basic beliefs and attitudes that
are often formed amid less demanding circumstances.
With their bland courtesy and effortless air of superiority,
the Chinese threw me back upon myself and made me
question everything. Sealed off so hermetically, I even

began to accept the Chinese view of themselves—not their political propaganda, but the Middle Kingdom outlook, the feeling that all the world revolves around Peking. Submerged amid this sea of blue, I began to doubt the relevance of my concerns and preoccupations. What did they matter, what did I matter, when compared to this vast drama that millions were playing all around me, with a disregard and indifference for my opinion that were almost total, and totally understandable? Cut off so completely from my own culture (which, to make matters much worse, I had never sufficiently explored or questioned), I had few guidelines to a saner outlook. Wondering at my own insignificance, I began to see myself as the Chinese must—loud, awkward, posturing, unreasonable, coarse, and selfish. Feeling drained and desiccated, I began to doubt my ability to love, my capacity for joy.

Then everything changed—not suddenly and dramatically, but slowly, with the seasons. And in the gentle rhythm of that change, I found new life and faith—in myself, and in Peking.

First came the torrents of spring, lashing the streets with sudden fury, washing away the winter's dust and then subsiding into bursts of azure sky. In the clear, sharp light, the solemn gray-stone walls and buildings were enlivened by the brilliant red of their arches, doors, and moon gates. Then summer, with lilacs in the courtyards, flowers on the Western Hills, and a dry heat that sent us, on the weekends, to find a shady solace beneath the Hunting Park's giant elms.

And for me there was romance, with someone who was equally a stranger, and equally haunted by Peking. It started on a sultry evening beside the Summer Palace lake. Free from its daytime hordes, the park was resting and at peace, with only a handful of Chinese walking or cycling along the paths. The air was soft against the face,

and in the stillness we heard the cry of birds, the chatter
of cicadas, and the comfortable smack of fishes jumping in
the limpid lake. A gray mist shrouded and softened the
contours of the somber Palace. With its intricate pictures,
the Painted Walk wound into the darkness; we almost
expected to meet the terrible Tzu Hsi, Old Buddha herself, taking her favorite walk, attended by other ghostly
shades of serving maids and eunuchs. In the distance the
Jade Fountain Pagoda loomed through the dark with two
red lights for eyes; it watched us like some benevolent sea
dragon, strangely marooned amid the hills, as we walked
together slowly through the dusk.

Perhaps to love a city, you have to love in that city. At
any rate, Peking was restored to me, and in that restoration I found new courage in myself and my instinctive
beliefs. That wise old Greek is right—in a sense every
perfect traveler does create the country where he travels.
So I made Peking in my own romantic image. This may
have been wildly unfair to the Pekinese, with all their
trials and vicissitudes. But great cities have more than
one reality, and I chose mine carefully.

I saw Peking again as I did, one evening early on, from a
rooftop looking out on the Forbidden City. That day there
had been a demonstration, and from the distance, we
heard the faint shrill of the whistles and the shout of the
slogans as the last of the marchers tramped back to their
homes. Gradually their clamor died, leaving the city to
itself, serenely surviving such transient concerns. Splendid
in their triumph, the gates and towers of the Great Within
stood outlined against the evening, blue-brown sky, and
cast their shadows on the soft waters of the moat. Directly
beneath us woodsmoke and the smell of suppers drifted
upward from the tiny, leafy courtyards. From somewhere,
perhaps inside the Palace walls, a solitary musician was

playing on a flute, piercing and poignant in the evening calm.

Another day, I stood in awe on the Altar of Heaven, beneath the brilliant sky to which the Emperors would make their annual obeisance. And I rejoiced, as I looked down the long open terrace, in the simple, blue-domed splendor of Heaven's Temple. With similar sensations of peace and reverence, I stood beneath the stupas, high atop the Temple of the Azure Clouds, wrapped between the green hills in a copse of silver pine which complemented the smooth white marble, so that suddenly I *knew*, in some way, how the Chinese feel for nature. And I honored that Chinese who built the place—an "infamous eunuch," according to one of the old guide books— for his infamies seemed less crucial than his lasting vision.

Something was reaffirmed. Once again it was good to wander in the crowds along the Wang Fu Ching, watching them throng to the watermelon stalls, devouring the great red slabs on the spot, juice running down their faces, spitting the seeds into the gutter. I ate the watermelon, too. Smiles were exchanged, something shared. Simple, perhaps, and probably naïve, my feelings. Yet in a way, a minor, undemanding way, it reassured me that for all my failures and frustrations, part of Peking would be mine forever. At the same time, I realized how much of China and the Chinese were still remote from me, would always be remote, but in what little I had loved and partly understood, I found contentment.

Then it was autumn, and the Western Hills were red and gold. There was a sharpness in the air, the markets were filled with orange mountains of persimmons, and from the Gobi there came the first fitful flurries of yellow dust. The cycle was complete; it was time to leave.

And so I went, with sorrow but no regrets. On that last morning we left early for the airport. In the dissipating darkness we wove our way through an army of carts and cyclists, trundling to their work. On the airport road the sun began to play on the crimson glory of the maple trees. And, a final irony, as we hurtled toward the sunrise, the East was most definitely red.

About the Author

CHARLES TAYLOR was the Far Eastern correspondent of the Toronto *Globe and Mail* from 1962 to 1965. For eighteen months he was based in Hong Kong, covering China and also visiting such countries as Japan, South Korea, the Philippines, Indonesia, Malaysia, Thailand, Cambodia, Laos, and South Vietnam.

For the next year and a half he lived in Peking, and his unusual experience as a resident in China's capital (as well as his travels to Canton, Shanghai, Harbin, Sian, Kunming, and many other places) is described in *Reporter in Red China*.

Mr. Taylor has also worked for Reuters, the Stratford Shakespearean Festival (Ontario), and as a free-lance writer and radio–television commentator from Europe, mainly for the Canadian Broadcasting Corporation.